C000109384

SHAKESPEARE: THE TRUTH

*The author contemplating Shakespeare's 'bust'
in London's Leicester Square*

PATRICK BARLOW

SHAKESPEARE:
THE TRUTH

OR
FROM GLOVER TO GENIUS

*Susie
with Thanks
Desmond Olivier Dingle
(author)*

BY
DESMOND OLIVIER DINGLE
with illustrations by the author

METHUEN

FOR SHEILA AND MORGAN

First published in Great Britain in 1993
by Methuen London
an imprint of Reed Consumer Books Limited
Michelin House, 81 Fulham Road, London SW3 6RB
and Auckland, Melbourne, Singapore and Toronto
First paperback edition 1994

Copyright © 1993 by Patrick Barlow
The author has asserted his moral rights

Photographs copyright © 1993 by Hanya Chlala

A CIP catalogue record for this book
is available at the British Library
ISBN 0 413 69260 4

Typeset by Rowland Phototypesetting Limited,
Bury St Edmunds, Suffolk
Printed in Great Britain
by Clays Ltd, St Ives plc

This book is sold subject to the condition
that it shall not, by way of trade or otherwise,
be lent, resold, hired out, or otherwise circulated
without the publisher's prior consent in any form
of binding or cover other than that in which
it is published and without a similar condition
including this condition being imposed
on the subsequent purchaser.

FOREWORD

by
The Author

I WISH this volume to be, not only a guide, manual and reference work, but also a deep source of inspiration. In which the Bard will speak to you, the Reader, *through me*, so to speak. I hope in fact that the two of us may become your Companions, if you will, on this mighty lifetime's journey, particularly during times of emotional or financial stress, which none of us are short of, needless to say.

In fact, it is my belief that only by repeatedly reading this book – and also *repeatedly buying it, in my opinion* – will you begin to feel its profound, not to say very special, effect. In other words, the more times you purchase this work, for your family, your colleagues, your children and your children's children, the more deeply will your life – not to say *their* lives – be irrevocably changed.

Not only for today – but for all time.

Thank you.

The Author

FORTHCOMING BESTSELLERS⋆
by Desmond Olivier Dingle

A Bard Too Far
Shakespeare's the Thing
Shakespeare and You
Shakespeare and Me
The Ascent of Shakespeare
The Shakespeare Problem (and How to Solve It)
O Shakespeare!
They Called Him Will
A Man Called Will
O Fatal Will
Make My Will – A Comedy
Lay on Shakespeare
Quill or Queen
The Shakespeare Diet
Shakespeare and Global Warming
Pole to Pole with Shakespeare
A Year with Shakespeare
Toujours Shakespeare!

⋆currently in preparation

CONTENTS

PART TWO
SHAKESPEARE: HOW TO DO IT

CONTENTS

LIST OF PLATES

PREFACE
'What manner of man was Shakespeare?'

OF all questions ever asked by the human race, 'What manner of man was Shakespeare?' is probably one of the most major.

In other words, how did he tick?

Did he experience the numerous minor complaints and various daily worries that many people ordinarily suffer? Such as the ordinary mortal cold, for instance?

Or was he somehow set apart from ordinary beings? Plucked out by Destiny so as he could create – without such things as common or garden worries or simple bodily ailments – his approximately fifty-seven collected works, seventeen sonnets and thirty-nine longer poems?

So do I know the answer to this fascinating query, i.e.:

'Who on earth was Shakespeare?'

And the answer is: I do.

In fact, it is astoundingly simple and yet profoundly true. And is as follows:

We have absolutely no idea.

And neither should we wish to. For the manner of man who was Shakespeare is a secret known only to the gods and the muses, and to his family and friends obviously, who possibly didn't know him either, so in point of fact nobody knew him, least of all himself, probably.

And so – having answered that – let us begin at last the mighty journey of this Œuvre. As we venture forth into the uncharted oceans of Shakespeareana itself to discover once and for all the object of our Grail.

Namely – *Shakespeare: The Truth!*

Thank you.

Desmond Olivier Dingle
November 1992

WARNING

Please note that the well-known play *Macbeth* is referred to throughout this work as 'The Scottish Play' for obvious reasons

SECOND PREFACE

FINALLY, before continuing any further with this volume, it is of course my momentous task, not to say privilege, to take this opportunity of acknowledging probably one of the greatest men in the world it has ever been my privilege to know.

I am, of course, referring to none other than Lord Methuen, without whose astonishing foresight, perseverance and courage, the book that you are currently holding in your hand *may well not have been published at all*!

Lord Methuen, of course, has chosen to live out his twilight years in his delightful residence on the South Coast, where – despite his occasional less than lucid moments – he still finds time to supervise his own personal selection of hand-picked 'works in progress', so to speak, from the Methuen headquarters or 'nerve-centre' in the Shady Pines Publishers Retirement Home, Bournemouth.

Fascinatingly, he only has two such works 'on the go' at the moment, a history of Swiss Cottage and mine. In other words a very *visionary* choice and one perhaps not always entirely to the taste of his London-based staff, who do at times have a tendency to become slightly surly, to be honest, particularly on the phone. Still, as I found myself saying to one young lady, only the other day, we can't have everything and it is surely only fair that his Lordship, who did after all found the entire Methuen Dynasty single-handed, should be allowed 'the two biggest jewels in the Methuen tiara' for himself.

Anyway, having been personally chosen by Lord Methuen, who I have not unfortunately had the honour of meeting, although certainly spoken to on the phone a couple of times – I would like to say that I believe his courageous decision to publish a work which threatens to rock the very foundations of Shakespearean scholarship quite a bit, will be one that neither he – nor Methuen's – will ever regret. Besides making everyone a few bob into the bargain.

And so it is with profound gratitude and the deepest humility that I dedicate this *œuvre* to Lord Methuen, who, once again, 'saw within me a flame no other man could see'.

Thank you, Your Lordship!

Desmond Olivier Dingle
May 1993

DEDICATED
to
LORD METHUEN BA

'He who ventured where others gained'

THIRD PREFACE

A ND so finally – let us recall the Bard's own immortal words:

> *'If I offend it is with our good will that you should think I come not to offend but with good will.'*

The meaning of which is not entirely clear, but certainly puts in a nutshell his intrinsic message, in my opinion.

Thank you.

Desmond Olivier Dingle
January 1993

PART ONE
A MAN CALLED SHAKESPEARE

'He yaf nat of that text a pulled hen'

(Chaucer)

CHAPTER I
THE BARD IS BORN
or
THE ROAD TO STRATFORD

'In the beginning was the end.'

(Holy Bible)

'Begin die ende zu beginnlich mein Enden
der begin der beguine.'

(Bismarck)

AND so it was, at the dawning of the Elizabethan Epoch, as it
was known – that a babe was born in a small well-known
English Midlands town called Stratford-upon-Avon[1] – home of
Anne Hathaway's Cottage, Mary Arden's House, Shakespeare's
Birthplace and the Royal Shakespeare Theatre Company.

And as his parents gazed down at that little new-born Elizabethan infant, his little Elizabethan ruff already round his little
rough Elizabethan neck, his little struggling Elizabethan body already clad in his first little all-in-one doublet and hose, and proudly
watched him mewling and puking all over his brand new little
Elizabethan duvet, they could not possibly have guessed what that
recently sired babe – fruit of their handiwork, so to speak – *would in
fact become.*

[1] Or Stratford East, Stratford-Atte-Bowe, Stratford Ontario or Stratford Johns, as
it was also known.

For the babe that lay before them – and already showing signs, *even as an infant*, of his famous prematurely receding forehead – was none other than that Son of Avon, the Immortal Swan himself, William Shakespeare.

In other words, the most famous man the world has ever known.

But who in fact was he?

Will we ever find out?

Or will he always remain 'shrouded in mystery'?

To answer these questions, and many more, we must now turn to Chapter II, 'Who Was William Shakespeare?'

The birth of Shakespeare

THINGS TO DO:

1. Make a scale model of ONE of the following:
i) 'The Dawning of the Elizabethan Epoch';
ii) Shakespeare's parents; iii) Shakespeare's parents siring Shakespeare; iv) Stratford Johns.

CHAPTER II
WHO WAS WILLIAM SHAKESPEARE?
or
A MYSTERY SOLVED

'Who was Shakespeare?'

Anon.

Introduction

William Geoffrey Shakespeare was born in Shakespeare's Birthplace in Stratford-upon-Avon but a stone's throw from Anne Hathaway's Cottage with whom he was to have a stormy and incestuous marriage in later years (see Chapter LXXXI, 'Later Years'[1]).

Summary of life

Unfortunately, this is all that is currently known of the extra-

[1] Anne Hathaway is also featured in our special feature – Chapter XVII, 'Shakespeare's Unknown Wives' – although, of course, Anne Hathaway was very much Shakespeare's *known* wife, and therefore only features in this feature sporadically. For further information on Anne Hathaway, see Chapter XCI, 'Anne Hathaway's Cottage – The Truth', and Chapter CXXIV, 'Anne Hathaway's Tearooms – Behind Closed Doors'.

ordinary and colourful life of William Shakespeare. Which leads us, of course, to the nub of this chapter. Not to mention this book.

Who was William Shakespeare?

In order to answer this, we need first to ask ourselves two further questions:

1. Who were his parents?
Although – as we have seen – nothing whatsoever is known about his parents, we *do* know, via combing through various records and so forth, that his father was George Shakespeare or possibly even Thomas Shakespeare, a well-known Elizabethan glove-maker from Stratford's Glove Quarter,[1] while his mother, of course, was Mary Arden, the popular Stratford cosmetics expert.

2. Did he get on with his parents, generally?
Yes, he certainly did. In fact, they never had any rows or suchlike, fortunately.

3. Why is that good particularly?
Because numerous other famous authors and what have you often have endless arguments and so forth with their parents which, as has now been proved via research, Shakespeare didn't have.[2] And finally:

4. Did Shakespeare's father's glove manufacturing influence Shakespeare's early works?
Yes, it certainly did. In fact, Shakespeare's early works are stiff with glove-manufacturing references, such as the memorable line from the well-known play *Richard II* who says 'He would unto the stews and from the commonest creature pluck a glove' – the actual meaning of which is unfortunately obscure (i.e. what the glove is actually doing in the stew is never fully explained) but does show both his fascination with gloves and an early familiarity with casserole cookery. In fact, many whole plays were inspired by his father's obsession with constantly inventing new kinds of gloves. In particular, the

---

[1] Or 'Compartment', as it was also known.
[2] Rows, that is, not parents, fortunately!

woollen glove which inspired *The Winter's Tale* (see Chapter III, 'Early Days in Sheep Street'), the measuring glove which inspired *Measure For Measure*, the animal-handling glove which inspired *The Taming of the Shrew* and, of course, the rubber glove which inspired *Pericles – Prince of Tyre*. And thus, Shakespeare got on extremely well with both his parents, fortunately.

Conclusion
Which, as I say, was a bit of luck for all concerned.

So what happened next in Shakespeare's extraordinary childhood?
To find out let us turn to the following chapter, 'Early Days in Sheep Street', and discover what happened next in Shakespeare's extraordinary childhood.

THINGS TO DO:

1. Paraphrase this chapter in the style of *Hamlet*.

2. Write a Revenge Tragedy finishing with the Shakespearean couplet:
    'My reindeer scents the Lapland snow;
    The sleigh-bells jingle; I must go,
    Leaving families round the fire
    Giving each his heart's desire.'

Some well-known gloves

ordinary glove

ski-ing glove (also oven glove)

evening glove

CHAPTER III

EARLY DAYS IN HENLEY STREET

'Inquire me first what Danskers are in Paris'

(Hamlet)

Introduction
This chapter was, of course, supposed to be called 'Early Days in Sheep Street' – as announced in the previous chapter (see last chapter). In the last few moments, however, I have just spotted – after a detailed reading of the well-known literary research work, *Stratford-upon-Avon – Shrine to a Genius*, price £1.95 – that Shakespeare's Birthplace is not actually in Sheep Street as such but in Henley Street, and so was, in fact, named after the Bard's mother Mary Arden. Whose *full name*, of course, was Mary Henley-in-Arden. Hence Henley Street.[1]

Sheep Street
Sheep Street, in fact, is actually some way from Henley Street and, although it does have an attractive selection of inexpensive restaurants and boutiques to suit all tastes, it doesn't have any actual Shakespearean monument on it at this juncture. Which explains

[1] Also Henley-on-Thames, Henley Regatta, Henley Bypass, Henley Police College and *Henry IV, Part 1.*

pretty cogently, in my opinion, why Shakespeare didn't actually live there.

Nevertheless, it was clearly a street full of sheep in its day and I am still convinced that this is where Shakespeare's father found the sheep which inspired the idea behind his famous 'woollen glove' which, of course, he not only invented but also sold worldwide.[1]

Sheep

There are, it has been estimated, at least seven hundred and eighty-seven references to 'sheep' in the *Complete Works of Shakespeare* which proves, in my opinion, that, although the Shakespeares didn't actually live in Sheep Street, Shakespeare himself was very used to sheep and had a lot of them in the house.

Also – fascinatingly enough – there are many references to the word 'sleep' in the Bard's works which are now generally believed to be a misprint for the word 'sheep' as well. 'Macbeth hath murdered sleep,' for instance, is much more likely to be 'Macbeth hath murdered sheep,' seeing as he was murdering everybody anyway so what difference would a couple of sheep make? Besides which 'murdering sleep' is an entirely meaningless expression.

I think I make my point.

Hence this chapter is called 'Early Days in Henley Street' and *not* 'Early Days in Sheep Street', as I'd intended to call it, having glanced, as I say, at *Stratford-upon-Avon – Shrine to a Genius* which, by the way, I can warmly recommend and is certainly well worth the price at £1.95.

Extraordinary Career

And so, having cleared that up with no hard feelings, let us continue our way through the colourful and extraordinary career of William Shakespeare.

Further Discoveries

Although, I would just like to mention a further discovery made by myself whilst on a recent 'day-trip' to Stratford-upon-Avon that I undertook for essential background research (see photographic section, 'A Journey Through Stratford-upon-Avon') which is basically this.

[1] Besides a number of other woollen items, such as the balaclava, the cardigan, the cashmere sweater and the fairisle tank top which were both fashionable *and* useful!

Sheep Street in Shakespeare's Epoch

A34

Why – when they have a perfectly good street actually called Shakespeare Street – did Shakespeare's parents not put the Birthplace there? Obviously, before the Bard's gifts had become fully evident, one could understand the Shakespeares not wanting to move the entire family across the A34 to what is, after all, not the most beautiful street in the world. However, once they realised they had a genius on their hands (and it's not every eighteen-month-old baby that wakes you up in the morning with a perfectly rendered second draft version of *Henry VI, Part 3* clutched in its little hand!), they should, in my opinion, have set up the whole Birthplace and Museum in the street which *at least bore his name*.

In other words and with no disrespect to his mother obviously, if you have a son who happens to be the Bard of Avon and a street in Stratford-upon-Avon called Shakespeare Street, then it seems to me pretty obvious you go for some sort of merging arrangement.

Because naturally, whatever one's interest – i.e. whether one is a mindless tourist or a bestselling literary expert, if one is on a trip to Stratford-upon-Avon and sees a street called Shakespeare Street one naturally presumes it'll have something in it, not a million miles from the object of one's Mecca, if you get my meaning. So it's somewhat upsetting to spend *at least an hour* of an extremely tightly scheduled coach trip legging it up and down what turns out to be totally the wrong street when, with a name like that, Sir Peter Hall himself could be forgiven for thinking it was the 'Bard's own street', so to speak.

So buck up, Stratford Council! Move the Birthplace Now! before it's too late! And before you lose any more valuable tourists! PUT THE BARD BACK WHERE HE BELONGS!!

THINGS TO DO:

1. Write short notes on the following: i) the A34;
ii) Mecca; iii) William Shakespeare; iv) Henley By-Pass;
v) Sheep.

2. Read *The Secret Diary of Sir Peter Hall* (pub. Hamish Hamilton, pr. £5.95 UK only) – this book changed my life!

3. Read *Stratford-upon-Avon – Shrine to a Genius* (pub. Unichrome (Bath) Ltd, Bath. Pr. £1.95). **WARNING:** Make sure you get the *English edition*. I spent a good half hour composing a letter to the publishers, complaining about illegibility, before realising I had in fact purchased the Japanese version, which is a mistake anyone could have made, seeing as the Japanese word for 'Shrine to a Genius' happens to be almost identical to the logo for English Heritage. Needless to say, I have no wish to reopen old wounds or cause any more of a rumpus than was caused at the time, except to say that the ensuing argument at the waxworks *considerably sullied* what would otherwise have been a thoroughly enjoyable, not to say, highly informative, 'trip through time', so to speak.

CHAPTER IV

SHAKESPEARE'S SCHOOLDAYS

'Gaudete vosque O Lydiae lacus undae; ridete quidquid est domi cachinnorum.'

(Anon. Meaning unknown.)

MEANWHILE it was time for Shakespeare's Schooldays to begin.

And not before time, if I may say so. And certainly not before writing Sonnets Numbers 1–37 as a special thank-you to his parents for getting on with him so well, for conceiving him in the first place and for reminding him it was time for his schooldays to begin.

Unfortunately, they weren't able to see him off, seeing as his mother was in Rome launching a new fragrance and his father in Zell-Am-See inventing a rudimentary ski gauntlet. However, they did leave him a packed lunch and a note to say they hoped everything would be all right.

And so – aged two and a half – William Shakespeare, with satchel on his back and shining morning face, although still occasionally given to mewling and puking everywhere, set off alone through the colourful and rumbustious streets of Stratford-upon-Avon and arrived three minutes later at the famous grammar school, Stratford-upon-Avon Grammar School, to experience for himself the harrowing privations of the English public school system.

Needless to say, within hours of his arrival, he had written three

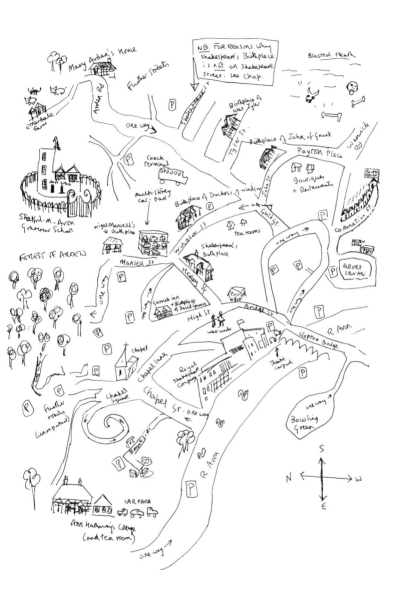

Illustrated map of Stratford-upon-Avon

of the most violent plays about schooldays every written, *Richard III*, *Titus Andronicus* and *Tom Brown's Schooldays* by Matthew Arnold. Nevertheless, life did have its lighter side and three days later he wrote *The Comedy of Errors* after being caned for a crime he didn't commit; *Love's Labours Lost*, after a day of heavy labouring; and *Much Ado About Nothing* about nothing in particular.

Meanwhile, besides writing his early Works, Shakespeare spent his schooldays studying Latin, Greek, needlework and logic, which was somewhat illogical, obviously, but that's the way it was in those days and who's to argue?

So did he learn anything else during his days at the grammar school?

Yes, he learnt grammar, obviously, but unfortunately that didn't go too well either.

Really?

Yes, extraordinarily, Shakespeare's grammar was so appalling that it's generally agreed it's amazing he ever got inside a publisher's foyer.

So is this, in fact, the main reason he is so hard to comprehend?

Do you mean why Shakespeare is so hard to make head nor tail of?

Yes.

Yes, it is, as a matter of interest.

Well, that is extraordinary!

What, that Shakespeare who wrote the greatest plays and sonnets known to man doesn't make any sense because of his appalling grammar?

Yes.

It certainly is. Let us look, for example, at an example of Shakespeare's appalling grammar:

> 'He that ears my land spares my team and gives me leave to inn the crop.'

Picked entirely at random from one of his least-known works, the well-known play *All's Well That Ends Well*[1] and written, admittedly, just after his seventh birthday and under appalling conditions of classroom flogging etc., it does, however, make no sense whatsoever, which is unforgivable, obviously, particularly given the fact that *All's Well That Ends Well*[2] is a play regularly viewed by audiences throughout the world, particularly foreign people, who surely have a right to a play they can at least understand – *or get the gist of if nothing else*!

Here is another example of Shakespeare's appalling grammar from another early work, *The Tempest*:

> 'If 'twere a kibe 'twould put me to my slipper.'

Again this means *absolutely nothing* and, in fact, only serves to confuse audiences throughout the world.

Obviously the odd nonsensical line is to be expected in a work of this length, but when a whole play is riddled with it, it's time to say, in my opinion, 'enough's enough'!

Which is exactly what Shakespeare's parents did as soon as they returned from the Continent.

They took one look at *The Tempest*, *As You Like It*, *Richard II* and *I Claudius* and removed him instantly from the premises.

Shakespeare's schooldays was at an end.

THINGS TO DO:

1. Describe in your own words: i) Richard II; ii) A Shakespearean packed lunch; iii) A kibe.
2. Translate four of Shakespeare's plays into one of the following: i) French; ii) Greek; iii) Morse code; iv) Logic.

---

[1] Also known as *Twelfth Night* or *A Little Of What You Fancy*.
[2] See Note 1.

CHAPTER V
EARLY DAYS

'The early tire gets the roofin' rack.'

(Anon.)

A ND so, aged nine and a half, Young Shakespeare – or Young Will as he was now known – left full-time education behind forever and immediately became a glover. Hence the well-known Shakespearean expression:

'And then the glover, sighing like Furnace, with woeful ballad made to his mistress eyebrow.'

This fascinating and much-loved quotation also reveals that Shakespeare – even at that early age – was a much travelled man and had, in fact, even visited the North of England. This we know, of course, from the reference to the name Furnace – or rather Barrow-in-Furnace, as it was known at the time.

Why?
Although why on earth he wanted to go to Barrow-in-Furnace, one can only guess, being one of the most hideous industrial spots in the entire world. Possibly he was visiting a relative in Grange-over-Sands.[1] Or even *en route* to the Lake District, seeing as he was a keen

---

[1] Both Barrow-in-Furnace and Grange-over-Sands, like Stratford-upon-Avon and Henley-in-Arden, are of course Elizabethan towns. How do we know this? And, more to the point, how do we spot it on the map, i.e. so we can inform fellow

fell walker and it's far more attractive, obviously.

And was also where he wrote a number of early works, including *Timon of Athens*, *The Maid of Buttermere*, *The Old Man of Coniston*, *Lady Winderemere's Fan* and *Fingal's Cave*.

Shakespeare en route to the Lake District

THINGS TO DO:

1. Write an essay telling us what the following expressions tell us about Shakespeare's England: i) Mistress eyebrow; ii) Roofin' rack; iii) Maid of Buttermere; iv) Shakespeare's England.

2. Make a fascinating simulated 'authentic Elizabethan map', by following the following EASY-TO-FOLLOW instructions below:
    a) Take one sheet of ordinary paper. Or vellum (preferably made from best goat or pig).
    b) Pre-heat oven.
    c) Boil kettle.
    d) Warm teapot.

---

passengers we are travelling through an Elizabethan town? Can you guess? Exactly. If it is 'in', 'upon', 'under', 'on', 'over' or 'le' something, then that town is always Elizabethan, e.g. Brompton-on-Swale, Poulton-le-Fylde, Newcastle-under-Lyme and Southend-on-Sea. Also 'double names', such as Hoyland Nether, Leamington Spa, West Bromwich, Tower Hamlets, and Scotch Corner. And, in fact, many ordinary or 'single-named' towns or hamlets, such as Southampton, Liverpool, Birmingham and London.

e) Make cup of tea (add milk and sugar as required).

f) Draw Elizabethan 'Map' on paper or vellum.

g) Draw in Elizabethan towns and Hamlets. Then various cherubs blowing wind and miniature trees, cows and shrubs and various inscriptions such as 'Here Be Dragons'.

h) Lightly beat wafer-thin gold leaf as decoration around edge.

i) Pour cup of tea over it. Wait till thoroughly soaked.

j) Put in oven. Leave forty minutes.

k) Remove from oven.

l) Leave to cool.

m) Put 'Map' in frame (preferably hewn from oak or elm of some three hundred year).

And – lo! – the perfect Elizabethan gift![1]

---

[1] And another reason for buying this book at Christmas! Although, needless to say, *Shakespeare: The Truth* is very much a 'timeless work' and therefore ideal for buying at any time, while the numerous attractive gift ideas throughout the book can be used for any occasion. Christmas would seem the most obvious one, obviously, but, as I say, it doesn't have to be Christmas. Particularly in countries that purchase this book but don't have Christmas.

CHAPTER VI

ROMANCE!

'Lhude sing cuccu!'

(Anon.)

A ND so – ten years later – Shakespeare's parents were amazed to see how much he had grown.

'How quickly he has grown,' said his mother, labelling another barrel of gentleman's aftershave.

'He certainly has!' replied her husband, trying on a pair of elbow-length evening gloves. 'Why, it seems only yesterday since he was nine.'

'Then is it not time he was wed?' asked his mother.

'It certainly is!' said his father.

'Not that we want to get rid of him.'

'Of course not! But wait!'

'What?'

'Frank Hathaway has a daughter as yet unwed.'

'He who manufactures the well-known marmalade?'

'No. He who runs the tearooms in Shottery.'

'You mean *Anne Hathaway*?'

'The selfsame.'

'But is she not about forty-eight?'

'Approximately. But she does have the cottage.'

'Anne Hathaway's Cottage!'

'Exactly.'

'We could do worse.'

'We could! Where is young Will?'

'Finishing off *King Lear*.'

'Not *still*!'

'Still sorting out the Goneril and Cornwall sub-plot in the second and third acts.'

'He hasn't sorted out the Goneril and Cornwall sub-plot in the second and third acts?'

'I'm afraid he hasn't.'

'Well, tell him to pack it in and leg it up the A422.'

'Shoot off to Shottery?'

'Exactly.'

'But upon what ruse?'

'Demand of him to take a selection of your latest gardening gloves for the Anne Hathaway gardens. Or, *better still*, an assortment of my latest toiletries and room-fresheners for the tearooms.'

'Within a week they will be wed!'

'And we don't have to pay!'

'Or go!'

'Fetch Will!'

And then suddenly, as if prompted by some deep inner prompting deep within themselves, they turned to the door.

For Will himself had appeared.

Instantly, the room was hushed. Even the colourful and rumbustious Stratford street outside fell to a strange unearthly silence and all one could hear was the pigeons in next door's dovecote and the simmering of his mother's deodorant vats. For a moment, all was quiet. And then, after gazing silently through the half-timbered latticework Tudor window, he slowly turned his finely chiselled, ruggedly handsome face towards his parents.

And, speaking unto them, he said, 'What wilt thou parents that thou dost call me thus?'

And they, replying unto him, replied, 'We was wondering if you might pop up to Shottery and deliver an assortment of gardening gloves and personal requisites to Mr and Mrs Hathaway of Anne Hathaway's Cottage.'

'Certainly, mine parents,' replied Young Will, 'but what is Shottery when it's at home?'

'Shottery is a minuscule hamlet on the A422,' replied his father.

There was the slightest pause.

'A minuscule what?'

'Hamlet.'

Instantly – without a second's in-drawing of breath – Shakespeare was gone.

Four hours later – his doublet all unbraced, no hat upon his head, his stockings fouled, ungartered and unpleasantly down-gyved – he reappeared and, slamming seven hundred pages down on the massive mahogany drop-leaf Elizabethan table, exclaimed, 'Not exactly a barrel of laughs, but it might just work! So anyway, what was it you was saying, mine parents?'

'We was wondering,' replied his father, still gasping at the full significance of having a First Folio edition of *Hamlet* in the living-room, 'if you might deliver a wide selection of gardening gloves and personal freshness products to the prosperous Hathaways.'

'And thus gain introduction to their well-known daughter and meet her with a view to marriage,' added his mother.

'Dost mean Anne Hathaway?' asked Will.

'Absolutely,' replied his parents.

'But is she not forty-eight or thereabouts?'

'Yes, but there is the Cottage to consider. Not to mention the tearoom.'

'But what if she will not wed me?'

'Where there's a will there's a way, Will,' said Shakespeare's father.

'True,' said his mother. 'Why not write *Romeo and Juliet* en route and give it to her as a gift.'

21

'Very well, mine parents, give me the box of samples and I will visit the preposterous Hiawathas.'

'Prosperous Hathaways.'

'Exactly.'

And so it was Young Will Shakespeare set off for Shottery[1] to meet her whose name shines next to his in many respects in the starry firmament of Shakespeareana and without whose unstinting support he would never have done half what he done.

THINGS TO DO:

1. Make a massive mahogany drop-leaf Elizabethan table.

---

[1] *WARNING:* Shottery, of course, not surprisingly, is often confused with Ottery St Mary, the deceptively dull Devonian market town famed for the ancient folk custom of Tar-Barrel Racing, in which teams from all over Devon get appallingly drunk on illegally brewed cider and hurl barrels of hot tar into the living-rooms of elderly residents. In fact, a number of people *en route* to Shottery have made this navigational error, including, as it happens, the Bard himself, which is why he took seven weeks to cover the mile-and-a-half journey from Shakespeare's Birthplace to Anne Hathaway's Cottage. And also myself, fascinatingly enough, due to an unfortunate mis-reading of the normally reliable AA Road Atlas.

CHAPTER VII
SHAKESPEARE'S MARRIAGE

'Como e para o bem de todos e a felicidade geral da nacao, estou pronto.'

(Pedro IV of Portugal)

A ND so, seven weeks later, Young Will Shakespeare arrived in
Shottery. And there it was, having tea and presenting his
toiletry items, that he first did glimpse Anne Hathaway. And she
glimpsed he also.

And once they had had tea and he had toured the house and
gardens, she took him to what was known as the 'wooing seat',
which all Elizabethan dwellings had, obviously, so that when
wooings occurred there was a seat to do it on, i.e. they didn't just
woo anywhere.[1] In point of fact, whilst I was personally on my own
tour of the house and gardens, during my recent researches into the
Life and Works of William Shakespeare, I myself was profoundly
moved to have the honour of actually sitting on the 'wooing seat'
myself.

An experience that was slightly marred, unfortunately, by the

[1] In fact, in Elizabethan times, one had to be extremely careful not to sit on the
wooing seat *by mistake*, i.e. if one didn't know what it was. Many was the weary
traveller, in other words, who would sit on one without realising it for a couple of
minutes before breakfast, only to find himself immediately and unaccountably
wooed in all directions and a married man by teatime. Things got so out of hand
that in 1607 all Guest Houses and Residents' Lounges were boycotted by travelling
salesmen until wooing seats were clearly marked by the Management.

fact that half of Utah State University appeared to be sitting on it as well. Without so much as an 'Excuse me, could I possibly shift up and give you a little more room on what is after all possibly the scene of the most intimate moment in Shakespeare's entire corpus?' In fact, one lady in a baseball hat, who wasn't exactly a sylph, if you get my meaning, had the entire wooing seat to herself for so long that the author of this work was forced to remind her there was a number of other people waiting to have a go on it as well, as it happened! Many of whom happened to be English, as a matter of fact, and therefore, in his opinion, and in a number of other people's opinions as well, in my opinion, had slightly more of a right to be there in the first place. Seeing as if it hadn't been for the English there probably wouldn't have even *been* a Shakespeare!

Anyway, when I was finally permitted to take my place on the courtship seat where Shakespeare first wooed Anne Boleyn, I can report that I did feel a strangely stirring *frisson*. A kind of glimmer, if you will, in parts of my loins, that I see no reason to go into at this juncture, but nevertheless left me very profoundly moved indeed.

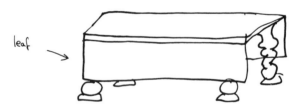

Massive mahogany drop-leaf Elizabethan table

To think that here it was that *Romeo and Juliet* was first heard, which he had, of course, been writing *en route*, to recite to her in its entirety as part of his wooing technique.

We can picture them now, can we not?

In those first moments of soft falling twilight. Will, Anne and three elderly chaperones all squeezed together as Shakespeare – or the burgeoning Bard as he had become known – declaimed on and on into the night.

Uttering some of the most deeply romantic words ever written:

'Away with the join-stools, remove the court-cubbert, look to the plate, good thou save me a piece of Marchpane and let the Porter let in Susan Grindstone and Nell, Anthony and Potpan.'

for instance, or:

'Take thou some new infection to thy eye,
And the rank poison of the old will die.'
'Your plantan leaf is excellent for that.'
'For what I pray thee?'
'For your broken shin.'
'Why, Romeo, art mad?'
'Not mad, but bound more than a madman is;
God-den good fellow.'
'God gi' god-den. I pray, sir, can you read?'

They wouldn't have understood a word of it, of course, particularly the elderly chaperones; but by the early hours of dawn her heart was his and by lunchtime they were married.

Unfortunately, Shakespeare's parents weren't able to be there, being away on various business conferences, but they sent them a large tub of facial cleanser, three pairs of mittens and a note to say they were sorry they couldn't be there and hoped everything would be all right.

Moments later, the newly-weds were escorted to their coach which was waiting in the coach park to begin the first journey of their life together, namely their honeymoon.

So why did Shakespeare get married?

In my opinion it is as if Shakespeare said unto the three Muses of Weddings, Psyche, Sybil and Clytemnestra, 'I am lonely and lost in my life, despite being a genius. Hearken to my call and give unto me a helpmeet to cleave unto me and be my bosom companion. For the agony of the creative being is a lonely one and one often longs for a partner and helpmeet in his afflictions. If you could see your way to giving me a hand in this regard, I would be more than grateful. Thank you.'

So let us now examine in detail where Shakespeare and Anne Hathaway might have spent their honeymoon.

THINGS TO DO:

1. Construct an Elizabethan 'wooing' seat:
   a) Saw three or four pieces of wood of various lengths.
   b) Hammer together, making large Elizabethan seat.
   c) Decorate with marvellously wrought carved scenes from classical antiquity, such as 'Cupid being Chased by Seven Sybils' and 'Lysander and Persephone Relaxing by a Pond'.
   d) Add arms.
   e) Varnish.

Fig. 1.
William Shakespeare and Anne Hathaway's wedding cake
(artist's reconstruction)

CHAPTER VIII

WHAT SHAKESPEARE AND ANNE HATHAWAY DID ON THEIR HONEYMOON

'If every man's internal care
Were written on his brow,
How many would our pity share
Who have our envy now.'

(Pietro Metastio –
Guiseppe Riconosciuto Part 1)

Introduction

One of the most intriguing dilemmas facing leading Shakespearean experts and artistic directors the world over is precisely how Shakespeare and Anne Hathaway spent their honeymoon.

Where?

Did they choose an English location,
in other words, or go for a
more exotic locale?

And, if so, where?[1]

Conclusion

So let us now, at this critical juncture of our tale of the Bard, examine in detail Shakespeare's age, if that's what everybody wants.

THINGS TO DO:

1. Write a short play, ending with Shakespeare having to break it to Anne Hathaway that they can no longer have a honeymoon.

2. Read a book on being an artistic director. NB Examples of a book on being a leading artistic director are:

All The World's A Globe – Desmond Olivier Dingle's controversial history of the Universe that also contains many fascinating insights into being a leading artistic director (pub. Mandarin, price £4.99).

The Secret Diary of Sir Peter Hall by Sir Peter Hall. Another fascinating glimpse into the life of a leading artistic director.

---

[1] I would just like to state, at this juncture, that I have just received what is known in publishing circles as a 'memo' from Lord Methuen with a number of suggestions concerning the current situation regarding choice of chapters. This is extremely helpful of him, obviously, but I must say I fail to see what he means when he says that, in his opinion, the reader isn't all that interested in where Shakespeare and Anne Hathaway went for their honeymoon. To which I would say, fair enough! I had personally thought they might be, but if everyone's finding it all appallingly tedious, then we can move on very easily and without any problem whatsoever to a totally different chapter of Lord Methuen's choice, if that's what Lord Methuen wants. His Lordship apparently believes it's about time we was having chapters entitled 'Shakespeare's Age' at this stage in the volume. To which all I can say is, all he has to do is say. I haven't been one of this country's leading artistic directors for nothing, if I may say so, and one of the first things one learns in this game is 'Always Keep One Step Ahead of Your Audience'. As any of our other leading artistic directors, such as Sir Peter Hall and Sir Richard Eyres and so forth, will tell you. Hence the ensuing chapter entitled 'Shakespeare's Age'. Although, as I say, it's no skin off my nose what we do.

CHAPTER IX

SHAKESPEARE'S AGE

'On us all doth haggish age creep on.'

(Shakespeare)

Introduction
So how should one begin with an examination of Shakespeare's age? And, more to the point, what exactly was it?

Shakespeare's Age
Unfortunately, it's a little difficult to know exactly how to give an answer to this rather odd question, but basically Shakespeare's age was Shakespeare's age. In other words, his age changed from year to year, as everybody's age changes, i.e. we all have a different age depending on what year it is.

Conclusion
In other words, to know how old anybody is all depends on what year you're talking about.

And Shakespeare was no exception.

THINGS TO DO:

1. Write short notes on the following: Shakespeare's Age.

1. Romeo

CHAPTER X
MARRIED LIFE

'She was prymerole, a piggesnye,
For any lord to leggen in his bedde
Or yet for any goods yeman to wedde.'

(Chaucer. Meaning unknown.)

AND so it was that Shakespeare and Anne Hathaway returned from their somewhat truncated honeymoon to live in Stratford in Shakespeare's Birthplace. Only to discover that, in their absence, Shakespeare's parents had opened not only both house and garden to the public, but also a small costume display and cosmetics counter. Needless to say, with a baby on the way and every room thronging with sightseers, it wasn't long before the cracks began to appear in the Shakespeare household, not to mention the Shakespeare house, which was only made of wattle and daub after all, and was already showing signs of subsidence.

The following day, the entire gable end collapsed into next door's garden and Shakespeare's parents moved immediately into Mary Arden's House in Wilmcote, where they invested the takings from the Birthplace and founded the Shakespeare Glove and Body Shop, before joining the Pilgrim Fathers and living in semi-retirement in Florida.

The following day, Anne gave birth to twins, a girl called Katharine and a boy called Hamnett. Meanwhile, things were getting desperate.

With barely a house to live in and another baby on the way, Shakespeare tried his hand at wattle and daubing but succeeded only in writing all four Problem Plays plus *Troilism and Cressida* in three and a half days. There was only one thing for it.

Will must get work.

So the following day, after finishing off *Coriolanus* to take his mind off things, he strode into the colourful and rumbustious streets of Stratford-upon-Avon and applied for whatever work he could get, which explains, of course, why there are so many different references to 'Job Opportunities' in his plays.

But – despite his willingness to try his hand at anything whatsoever – things were more desperate still. The twins were getting bigger, the new baby never smiled and still they couldn't find the right consistency for the wattle and daub.

There was only one thing for it.

Will must go to London and make his living as a playwright.

'Go to London, Will!' said Anne, 'and make thy living – as a playwright!'

'But what about you?' exclaimed Will, packing his bags instantly.

'What about me?' she exclaimed.

'What about the twins and the wattle and daub and our new grim-faced baby?'

'Never mind about me and the grim-faced baby,' she said grimly. 'Leave me to achieve the right wattle and daub consistency. This is your destiny, Will Shakespeare. Now go before I drop tears as fast as the Arabian trees their med'cinable gum.'

The Shakespeares

And so, pausing a moment to jot that down to use it later in *Othello*, he embraced her and the grim-faced baby briefly, then turned towards London.

'Give my regards to the twins,' he said.

'Give my regards to Broadway,' she replied somewhat bitterly.

'I will,' said Will.

'And Will –' she said.

But Will was gone.

Striding into the early evening mist that swirled around him and instantly enswathed him and hid him finally from view. And on and on he went through the hushed Stratford streets towards the attractive and historic Clopton Bridge, heading for the A34 and London.

Modern-day London

THINGS TO DO:

1. Write an essay describing what you would do with the following: A Water-Rug; Long Purples; Vulcan's Stithy; A Sterile Promontory; A Muse of Fire; Black Vesper's Pageants.

2. Respond briefly to the following well-known Shakespearean commands:
'Off, off, you lendings!'
'Ha, ha, ha!'
'Pish!'

CHAPTER XI

THE LOST YEARS OF SHAKESPEARE:
A LITTLE-KNOWN FACT

> *'And there are also many other
> things which Shakespeare did,
> the which, if they should be
> written every one, then even
> the world itself could not
> contain the books that should
> be written, probably.'*

(Anon.)

AND then – all of a sudden – the trail unaccountably stops. Shakespeare, in other words, suddenly vanishes.

But where? And – more important – why? And how?

We last saw him – the reader will recall – striding towards the mighty Avon with nothing but his quill and a change of tights onto that marvel of Elizabethan bridge construction, the attractive and famed Clopton Bridge, designed of course by Isambard Kingdom Buñuel – the well-known surrealist ship and bridge builder.[1]

---

[1] N.B. One of the first laws passed by Henry VIII and one that radically improved the lot of Elizabethan England a lot, in fact, was the law that those who did the ships *also did the bridges*, e.g. Buñuel. And this was for a very simple but essential

So what had happened? Where had he got to? And why was there suddenly no record of his whereabouts?

Needless to say, his family were desperate. As they scoured the lanes and the byways, the hutments and the hostelries, the teashops, taverns, hamlets and shylocks. But still no sign of that strange young man, with his haunted expression and prematurely receding hair-line. Was it, in fact, *that*, they wondered, that had caused him to 'go to ground'?

The famed Clopton Bridge in Elizabethan times

---

reason that in the Epoch previous to the Tudor Epoch, bridge builders didn't do the ships as well and therefore bridges were always built too low (usually as a result of skimping on struts) thus making the sinking of essential shipping tragically commonplace. Many, in fact, were the tiny Elizabethan riverside hamlets whose inhabitants lay abed nightly in their little Shakespearean four-posters just counting the minutes before the next colossal galleon slammed into the inadequately strutted bridge that they knew ONLY TOO WELL was too low.

So the new law that insisted that bridge and boat building was all put under the same roof, or in the same boat so to speak, brought an enormous degree of relief to all concerned, not least the miniature Elizabethan riverfolk.

Because his hair was distressing him?

Or rather his lack of hair?[1]

Or is there possibly another reason? A deeper reason, why at this point in our story Young Will suddenly vanishes?

I believe there is.

I believe, in fact, that during the 'Lost Years of Shakespeare' or 'Shakespeare's Hidden Years' as they are known Shakespeare was nowhere near the Clopton Bridge or even the A34.

It is my belief that Shakespeare was in fact in Tibet.

Tibet! I hear the reader exclaim.

Yes, believe it or not, I believe Shakespeare was in Tibet.

But why would Shakespeare go to Tibet?

Why was he there?

Yes, why was he there?

He was there – I believe – to study essential spiritual truths and rehearsal techniques.

But surely such a journey would have been highly dangerous to an up-and-coming playwright?

I take your point but, on the other hand, we know that the Bard was never happier than when engaged in situations involving extreme danger, i.e. constantly pushing his physical limitations to the utmost of their bodily endurance.

How?

I beg your pardon?

How do we know this then?

We know this via Tudor records which prove beyond a shadow of a doubt that Shakespeare was only truly content when living on the razor's edge.

– no stranger to danger in other words?

---

[1] Readers who may be interested in Shakespeare's well-known hair loss difficulty should refer to the controversial photographic section, 'Shakespeare's Hair Loss Difficulty'.

Exactly.

So where are the records, exactly?

In a number of special governmental Tudor records offices in a secret bunker beneath the Tottenham Court Road.

But how do we know the Bard didn't finish up in Tibet by mistake? With map-making in its infancy, it would be an easy error to make.

To finish up in Tibet without meaning to?

Exactly.

Yes, it is certainly a possibility. It is, in fact, known that a number of Tudors did finish up in Tibet by mistake, such as the Duchess of Malfi and Lord Howard of Effingham.

Really?

But despite this I believe that Shakespeare knew EXACTLY WHERE HE WAS GOING. In fact, I believe that after he crossed the Clopton Bridge in 1491, he DID NOT take the A34 to London as was previously thought and AS HE HAD TOLD HIS WIFE AND FAMILY but in fact secretly took the A1071 to Harwich and from thence to Oslo. In Oslo he received a false passport and joined a camel train to Minsk. From Minsk he received a false beard and took a caravan to Gdansk – a lightweight touring caravan, as it happens, or rather, a small caravanette – and then from Gdansk to Khartoum, from Khartoum to Hong Kong, from Hong Kong to Melbourne, from Melbourne to Auckland. And from Auckland, of course, a simple hop to Tibet. By nightfall – the land of the Llamas lay within His grasp.

That is extraordinary.

Yes, it certainly is.

And something not many people know about.

Absolutely.

Anyway, what happened then?

Unfortunately, it is hard to say exactly what happened then. Seeing as Tibet is a very secret place, as is well known.

2. Famous Elizabethan Dances 1:
The gallimauphrey

Fair enough. But is it your belief that the Bard of Avon spent a number of years walking the length and breadth of Tibet, studying essential spiritual truths and rehearsal techniques?

It is, in fact, yes.

Such as Warm-Up Games and suchlike?

Exactly.

And the Stanislavski System?

I beg your pardon?

The Stanislavski System?

Yes, it is my belief that Shakespeare very much also discovered the Stanislavski System in Tibet.

So what actually led you to this remarkable discovery?

Well, to begin with, everything was fine. And then – little by little – I started discovering a number of things that JUST DIDN'T ADD UP.

You mean they just didn't make sense?

That's exactly what I mean.

Good Lord. Well, that seems pretty conclusive.

Well, I certainly think so.

And finally what is the Stanislavski System, precisely?

Unfortunately I am not in a position to examine the Stanislavski System in the necessary depth it requires at this precise juncture.

But there will be a larger chapter in this volume very much analysing and examining the Stanislavski System in precise detail later?

Very much so, I'm happy to say.

Thank you.

Thank *you.*

SHAKESPEARE: THE TRUTH

THINGS TO DO:

1. See the legendary feature film *Khartoum*.
2. Outline the following briefly: i) Lord Howard of Effingham; ii) Oslo; iii) The Stanislavski System.

Tibet

CHAPTER XII

THE LOST YEARS OF SHAKESPEARE:
A PROBLEM SOLVED

*'That which is now a horse
the rack dislimns.'*

[Lester Piggott]

There is one thing I find slightly worrying, however.

Oh yes?

Why do Shakespeare's barefoot Tibetan journeyings never feature in any of his thirty-seven plays and sonnets?

This is a good question, and one I am often asked. The reason is, I believe, that Shakespeare quite simply *forgot he'd ever been there.* And the reason for this is that Shakespeare had what is known medically as a *fugue.*

So what is a fugue when it's at home?

Fugues is what happens to people when they forget what's happened to them. As a result of a traumatic incident such as being a serial killer, for instance, which is generally a thing one tends not to want to be and therefore one would tend to forget that one was, obviously.

41

Although presumably you're not suggesting that Shakespeare harboured anything remotely approaching a deviant gene.

I'm certainly not.

How could someone who wrote, 'Sleep nae mo'e oh wandering brook, fair gang the times awa' 'possibly have had psychotic tendencies, let alone stoop to serial slaying, in other words?

Exactly!

Well that's a relief.

It certainly is.

THINGS TO DO:

1. State whether you have ever had any of the following: i) a *fugue*; ii) a *toccata and fugue*; iii) an *augmented fifth*; or iv) a *quaver*?
Which was worse?

2. Beware the Ides of March.

CHAPTER XIII

SHAKESPEARE COMES TO LONDON

*'Als Shakespeare wird 1592 erstmals seine Verbindung zum London
    erwähnt 1594.'*
    [Shakespeare came to London in 1593, approximately.]

(*Stratford-upon-Avon – Shrine to a Genius*, German Ed.
Pub. England's Glory Pamphlets, Chelmsford, Ltd.)

A ND so it was, that as the young Bard crossed Muswell Hill and
approached Tower Bridge, he must have felt one of the most
massive surges of excitement ever felt in the history of World
Literature. For there before him was his first colourful and rumbustious vista of St Paul's Cathedral, Oxford Street and Tottenham
Court Road. In other words – London! Or 'ol' Lunnun Town' as it
was known. In other words, Shakespeare's life – though he could not
have known it at the time, obviously – *would never be the same again.*

So what was London in fact like in the Tudor Epoch?

In order to answer this fascinating question, I have decided to
experiment with a form of historical research that I believe has not
been used in any previous autobiography until this volume.

Namely, via self-hypnosis.

Or – to be more specific – by hypnotising oneself into a deep
trance-like state via *self-hypnosis* and thus meeting numerous people
who one has in fact *actually been* in various past lives. So that, by

43

talking to them, or rather talking *to oneself*, one can learn exactly how life would have been at the time from the horse's mouth, as it were.

And so – via this fascinating and little-known technique – let us take a unique time trip back through time itself and visit Shakespeare's London *as Shakespeare himself would have seen it*.

In the company of someone who – believe it or not – *I myself once was*! Back in the Tudor Epoch some seven or eight hundred years ago, approximately. In fact, the perfect guide to the streets of London Town. A colourful and rumbustious cockney coster. Or 'sparrer' as they – or rather I – was known.

To witness this fascinating experiment, please turn to the ensuing chapter.

Colourful and rumbustious London

THINGS TO DO:

1. Write short notes on the following London expressions: i) costers; ii) Tottenham Court Road; iii) gang the times awa'; iv) self-hypnosis.

44

IMPORTANT WARNING TO ALL READERS

On no account attempt self-hypnosis without proper training and a deep inner self-knowledge. Discoveries CAN BE SHOCKING and self-hypnotees SHOULD BEWARE OF UNPLEASANT RESULTS IF ATTEMPTING WITHOUT THOROUGH GROUNDING IN CORRECT TECHNIQUES. These include irreversible psychic damage, such as inability to escape from past-life state or 'Confused Epoch Syndrome'.

END OF WARNING

CHAPTER XIV
A GLIMPSE INTO SHAKESPEARE'S LONDON:
A FASCINATING 'TIME-TRIP'

'In fair Verona where we lay our scene.'

(Shakespeare)

I understand you are the perfect guide to the streets of London Town. A colourful and rumbustious cockney coster. Or 'sparrer' as they was known.

Yes, that is correct.

So what was Shakespeare's London in fact like in the Tudor Epoch?

Unfortunately, very little is known about Shakespeare's London in the Tudor Epoch owing to the terrible loss of records that kept occurring, on account of the Plague that was regularly ravaging through everything and thus destroying records. This, of course is a tragic loss but it would be a mistake to apportion the blame to Londoners. In other words, if you was suffering from the Plague and suddenly everyone was coming round your house singing 'Bring Out Your Dead' and 'Ring a' Ring a' Roses', the last thing you'd want to do was keep records.

So it's hardly surprising you didn't have any, in other words?

Exactly.

So do we in fact know anything of Shakespeare's London in the Tudor Epoch?

Well, we do know that it was considerably smaller than it is in your epoch.

How fascinating! So what did it consist of, then?

It consisted of Hyde Park Corner, Crouch End, West Hampstead and the Holloway Road.

And what about other well-known Elizabethan or Shakespearean venues such as Aldgate, Ludgate, Cripplegate, Cheapskate, Bishop's Stortford and Pudding Lane? Were they not also in Shakespeare's London of the Tudor Epoch?

Yes, they most certainly were, and very much so, if I may say so.

So where precisely were they?

What?

Aldgate, Ludgate, Cripplegate, Cheapskate, Bishop's Stortford and Pudding Lane?

Unfortunately, owing to various problems such as 'record loss' (outlined above) it is impossible to pinpoint their exact locations with any degree of accuracy.

So were they very colourful and rumbustious?

Yes, they were in fact extremely colourful and rumbustious.

So what do you actually recall of the colourful and rumbustious world of Tudor London?

Unfortunately, that is in fact all that is known as at this precise juncture.

Well, thank you for a most fascinating and informative 'time trip'.

Thank you.

Goodbye. Or rather, wotcher mate!

Wotcher mate.

THINGS TO DO:

1. Write an essay outlining any past lives you might have had, answering the following questions:
i) How come you are so sure?
ii) On what do you base your evidence?
iii) Would it stand up in a Court of Law?

N.B. If the answers to these questions are likely to be as follows:
i) On second thoughts, I'm not particularly;
ii) Nothing really;
or
iii) No, it wouldn't, probably;

DO NOT PROCEED.

CHAPTER XV

FIRST DIGS!

'Death is working like a mole,
And digs my grave at each remove.'

(George Herbert)

The search begins!

So what did the Bard do after he arrived in Tudor London?

The first thing he did, of course, was search for digs but, although the capital did have a number of digs, there was a massive dearth of 'theatrical digs', unfortunately, which the Swan of Avon very much needed for obvious reasons.

Dearth of digs

The reason for this, of course, was due to the massive dearth of theatres. Owing to the fact that they hadn't actually started yet and thus causing – not surprisingly – the worst case of 'West End doldrums' yet known. In other words, when audiences jadedly exclaimed, 'There's absolutely nothing on in the West End,' they'd never spoken a truer word.

Awards

Let us, in fact, pause a moment and take a random glance at some of the categories of a typical Tudor Olivier Awards Ceremony, show-ing the 'all-time low' to which things had sunk:

* Most Sturdy Beggar
  Presented by: Jane Seymour

* Best Unicyclist
  Presented by: Sir Walter Raleigh

* Least Offensive Dancing Bear Act
  Presented by: Philip II of Spain

* Best Tumbler
  Presented by: The Thane of Cawdor

* Best Lady Tumbler
  Presented by: Samuel Pepys

* Most Promising Tumbling Foursome
  Presented by: Ivan the Terrible

* Least Unfunny Routine Involving Pig's Bladder
  Presented by: The Convocation of Canterbury

* Special Award for Continuing Furtherance of British Oral Tradition
  Jointly presented by Pope Innocent III and Margaret of Burgundy

Digs at last!

But Shakespeare did not despair, and it wasn't long before he found the perfect theatrical digs. The only drawback being that they were in Morecambe, which made commuting somewhat difficult owing to the rudimentary coach service but did introduce him to a host of other 'young hopefuls', including Francis Durbridge, Philip Marlowe, Ben Jonson and Samuel Johnson,[1] Beaumont and Fletcher, Lilley and Skinner, and Ralph Roister-Doister.

Immediately, after a hearty breakfast of Lancashire Hot Pot, the bevy of burgeoning dramatists became firm friends and, setting up their own itinerant theatre company, set off to sell their wares in the nation's throbbing capital.

For a few days all went well and then – quite suddenly – a problem arose.

---

[1] Or Jonson and Johnson, as they became known. Famed, of course, for their rumbustious comedies, baby oil and varied assortments of elasticated band-aids.

Problem!

They realised that they'd spent so long arguing over who had the biggest room and whose turn it was to do the washing-up after the Lancashire Hot Pot that not one of them had lifted so much as a quill in the last six months. In other words, they had totally run out of plays! What were they to do? Things were at breaking point.

A solution had to be found!

Solution!

Fortunately, however, the five pals came up with the perfect solution. They would collaborate on a number of well-known plays and take the West End by storm.

For a while, the collaboration went swimmingly. And then, suddenly, another problem arose.

Another Problem!

They all started arguing again, this time over each other's bits. Particularly, *whose were the best bits*.

Once again – things were at breaking point.

Three days later, Jonson and Johnson turned to drink; Beaumont and Fletcher went off in a huff; Ralph Roister-Doister became a chartered accountant; and Lilley and Skinner murdered Philip Marlowe under the Deptford flyover after an argument over the Dactylic tetrameter. Shakespeare was close to despair.

But a solution was near at hand. An even better solution, in fact, than the last solution.

Morecambe Bay

He decided to sit down at his little rollmop Elizabethan writing desk in his tiny little garret overlooking Morecambe Bay and write his audience a *new kind of play*. A play to transport them into the heart, not of Athens, or Venice, or even fair Verona, but their own 'flower of cities', London Town herself.

He would write his well-known 'London Plays'.

For a while, however, he was still close to despair. In fact, even closer to despair than he was the last time. Play after play burst from his quill: *Othello – Moor of Venice*, *Hamlet – Prince of Denmark*, *Two Gentlemen of Verona*, *Timon of Athens*, *Birdman of Alcatraz*, *Seagulls over Sorrento*, *Monte Carlo – or Bust*. But none was quite right.

None, in other words, a true 'London Play'.

Thank goodness!

And then at last, one night, *just as he had nearly given up*, he looked down at the play he'd just completed. And there in the flickering candlelight he realised he had written one of the most famous plays about London he had ever written – *The Merry Wives of Windsor*. Or rather *The Merry Widow* as it was more popularly known.

Full Examination

So, without more ado,[1] let us turn to the following chapter for a full examination of this famed play. And, in particular, *how come he wrote it.*

Shakespeare's first 'digs'

Conclusion

Finally, where did all those other so-called emergent playwrights of the Bard's Early – or 'Morecambe' – Years actually go? Did they ever come back to explain?

---

[1] Not to be confused, of course, with *Further Ado*, the shortened title of Shakespeare's famous uncompleted sequel to *Much Ado* or *Much Ado About Nothing*. In *Further Ado About Nothing*, the same characters find themselves getting into even more scrapes than last time!

Or even apologise?

Or did they simply vanish? Never to be heard of again?

The answer – in Shakespeare's own immortal words – is 'nasty, brutish, short and not overly pleasant but nevertheless *has to be said*'.[1]

Lilley and Skynner

We don't know and *we don't actually care*.[2]

THINGS TO DO:

1. Describe how you would answer the following Shakespearean questions:
   a) Who would fardels bear?
   b) What bloody man is that?
   c) How now, my headstrong, where have you been gadding?
   d) What trade art thou feeble?
   e) Woo't drink up esill?

2. Write short notes on the following: London; Transport; London Transport; Monte Carlo; Bust.

[1] His italics.
[2] My italics.

CHAPTER XVI
THE MERRY WIVES OF WINDSOR
THE STORY BEHIND A MASTERPIECE

'Would he bare his fardels?'

(Shakespeare)

B efore examining this fascinating play, it is important firstly to ask, 'Where is Windsor?'

And the answer, of course, is just off the M4. In other words, *not actually in London, as such.*

So can one actually call it a 'London Play', given this startling new evidence?

To which we can say, thank goodness, 'Yes, we certainly can!' Seeing as – and not many people realise this – Windsor has, in fact, only been on its present site since 1953, when the Royal Family decided to make it a Royal Residence. And, in fact, moved the whole Castle and Safari Park etc. *out of* London, where it had been originally, to make room for their own 'merry wives'. In other words, Princess Margaret, Princess Anne, the Princess of Wales, the Duchess of York and Captain Mark Philips, none of whom are very merry any more, unfortunately, or rather, *are* merry, but not in Windsor.

In fact, Windsor nowadays is probably one of the least merry places in the entire world, regarding wives. But that doesn't mean to say that Her Majesty the Queen and Prince Philip who, I am delighted to announce, are still very merry indeed – and very *actively* so, if I may say so – aren't still *absolutely delighted* with their 'move down the M4', as it is still known in Royal Circles.

So anyway if Windsor wasn't in Windsor, basically, where in fact was it?

Do you mean the Windsor in Shakespeare's Epoch?

Yes, the Windsor in Shakespeare's Epoch.

Well, fascinatingly, the Windsor in Shakespeare's Epoch was in fact just off the Strand.

Really?

Yes.

So what is now just off the Strand was then the Borough of Windsor?

No, in fact, it was the Borough of Slough, which Windsor is in, of course.

So the Borough of Slough was in fact just off the Strand?

Yes.

So The Merry Wives of Windsor *should in fact be called* The Merry Wives of Slough?

Exactly.

So why did the Bard not call his play The Merry Wives of Slough?

Unfortunately, we can only hazard a guess at this intriguing and oft-asked query, but probably because *The Merry Wives of Slough* doesn't have quite the same ring to it.

So, anyway, who exactly were the Merry Wives?

The Merry Wives of Windsor?

Absolutely.

Or rather *Slough*, obviously?

Yes.

Well, Windsor, fascinatingly enough, was, in fact, chiefly famous as a massive Tudor 'dating area'.

Good heavens. So what does that mean then? That the whole area was chock-full of wives? And men from all over Europe went there in order to find one?

Exactly.

Good heavens. So presumably young Will could barely believe his eyes?

Exactly.

Johnson and Jonson

As he wandered innocently out of Trafalgar Square, down the Strand and into Slough – only to find himself accosted by thousands upon thousands of wives all merrily larking about and giving him the eye and so forth.

Very much so, if I may say so.

So it is not surprising, in other words, that he wrote probably his most famous play The Merry Wives of Windsor *as a direct result of this experience?*

Yes, and furthermore, that Shakespeare took unto himself a number of further wives also as a result.

Good heavens! So how many exactly?

Unfortunately, I am not at liberty to say at this juncture, but suffice it to say quite a few.

So who were they then, these further wives?

The exactly identity of Shakespeare's further wives is, unfortunately, not known. Hence they are now termed Shakespeare's Unknown Wives.

THINGS TO DO:

1. Rewrite this chapter as a Petrarchan Sonnet.
2. Make a fardel.

WARNING TO TEACHERS

The following analysis of Shakespeare's Unknown Wives is very much an adult analysis and describes certain aspects of Shakespeare's private life, in uncompromisingly explicit and forthright terms.

★ SPECIAL FEATURE!!! ★

CHAPTER XVII

SHAKESPEARE'S UNKNOWN WIVES

'I've rarely seen such fardels.'
(Chaucer – *The Wife of Bath*)

Introduction
So, as I was saying, the exact identity of Shakespeare's Unknown Wives is unknown.

Conclusion
Although it is generally agreed by Shakespearean and marital experts throughout the world that this is probably just as well, all things considered.

But how can we be sure?
In other words, how can we be one hundred per cent absolutely certain that Shakespeare *had all these wives?*

And the answer to this critical but fascinating query is, of course, as follows.

We look at the text
Not only of Shakespeare's most famed play of all time *The Merry Wives of Windsor* but of all his plays, i.e. *every play he ever wrote.*

3. Four Shakespearean heroines:
Lady Macbeth; Titania;
Juliet; Another Famous Heroine

So what happens then?
We are instantly struck by one incontrovertible feature.

An incontrovertible feature?
Exactly.

So do we need to be an expert to spot this incontrovertible feature or can anybody spot it?
You need to be an expert to *get the idea* of spotting it, but not to actually *spot it*. In fact, you can spot it in the *comfort of your own home*, believe it or not.

So what exactly is it we're spotting?
Namely, that in the works of Shakespeare, the word 'wife' appears one hundred and fifty-four times, the word 'wedding' six hundred and thirty-seven times and the word 'marry' a staggering two thousand, seven hundred and fourteen times. Such as:

> 'Does he lie at the garter? Ay marry, does he?'

or

> 'What, quotha? Ay, marry grammercy!'

or

> 'Gloster is dead, marry, God forfend!'

Which actually tells us what when it's at home?
That as soon as he left Anne Hathaway and the twins, Shakespeare became *obsessed with marrying a number of further wives.*

Conclusion
And is in fact also why he wrote Shakespeare's other well-known 'Wife Plays', *The Wife of Bath*, *The Brides in the Bath*, *The Bride of Fu Manchu* and *I Married the Mob*, which are full of numerous wives, such as Anne Boleyn, Princess Anne, Anne of Green Gables and Katherine Mansfield.

The Brides in the Bath

So finally, how did I come up with this extraordinary evidence?

By simply reading *every Shakespeare play he ever wrote* until the evidence was too incontrovertible to miss, basically.

THINGS TO DO:

1. Make another three fardels.

CHAPTER XVIII
THE GLOBE IS BORN

'All the world's a globe.'

(Desmond Olivier Dingle)

WITHIN days, William Shakespeare was performing his plays to massive crowds in Covent Garden's world-famous piazza.

But – almost immediately – a problem presented itself.

Hardly anyone could see.

As a result, riots broke out, London was in uproar and the Bard close to despair.

And then – one day – an idea was born.

Probably the most audacious idea he had ever had since writing *The Merry Widow* in Morecambe. But, nevertheless, one that *might just work.*

He – William Shakespeare, Bard of all Avon – would build the Globe Theatre!

The first of many theatres to be built in London's fabulous 'Theatreland' – or West End obviously. Or rather East End, as it was known at the time.

But how on earth could he – a penniless playwright wandering the thronging backstreets of Cheapskate and Leicester Square full of rumbustious colourful street vendors, wits and gossips and so forth – build a massive theatre?

Whenever he suggested it to the various street vendors, wits and gossips and so forth, however, they all simply laughed.

'Build the Globe Theatre?' they quipped. 'Pull the other one!'

But Shakespeare was not to be deterred. *For he knew exactly what to do.*

He must discover a Patron.

But where?

WHERE ON EARTH COULD SHAKESPEARE
DISCOVER A PATRON?

To discover where Shakespeare discovered a Patron, turn to the following chapter, 'Shakespeare Discovers a Patron'.

THINGS TO DO:

1. Discover a Patron.

The World in Shakespeare's Epoch

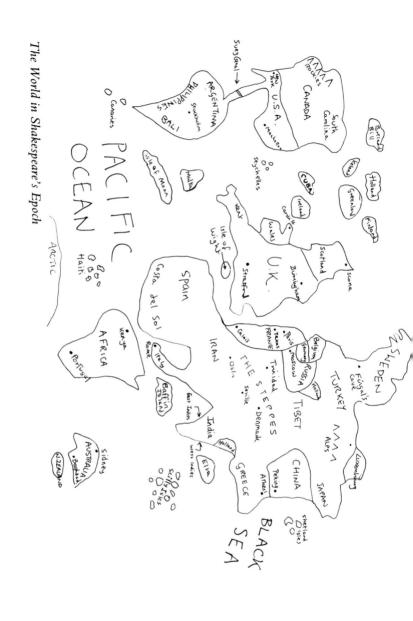

CHAPTER XIX

SHAKESPEARE DISCOVERS A PATRON

'While the train rolled onward,
A husband sat in tears
Thinking of the happiness
Of just a few short years.'

(Shakespeare)

Discovering a Patron

The only way a theatre company could ever get off the ground in the Tudor Epoch was by discovering a Patron. And not any old Patron, obviously, but a noble Patron, i.e. a noble. In other words, it simply wasn't worth having a Patron if he wasn't a noble.

The problem with discovering a Patron

The problem with discovering a Patron, however, tended to be that most theatre companies were generally made up of rogues, vagabonds and Sturdy Beggars, a type of person who most nobles didn't get on with, unfortunately. Hence it was very difficult being a vagabond or Sturdy Beggar and finding a Patron.

The other problem with discovering a Patron

The other problem with discovering a Patron, of course, was that nobles were generally only interested in fox-hunting and dancing the gallimauphrey and not remotely interested in small itinerant fringe companies of Sturdy Beggars doing devised plays about housing. Nevertheless, the Sturdy Beggars were not to be deterred. And it's a bit of luck they weren't! For without them the theatre as we know it *might never have occurred.*

So how did they discover nobles, then?

Generally, the Sturdy Beggars' theatre companies would set up by the roadside of a well-known road or route known to be frequented by nobles, such as just outside Longleat on the A362 or *en route* to Blenheim Palace on the A34, for example. And here – in all weathers – they would perform their disgracefully unsponsored dramas.

Another problem with discovering a Patron

Another problem with discovering a Patron of course was that quite often the nobles would gallop by in their coach after a point-to-point or whatever and not actually *see* the Beggars. Due to the fact that the Beggars – not having any costume budget – were so drab in appearance that they totally blended in with the grass verges. Which are not overly colourful at the best of times, particularly in the West Midlands.

A bit of luck, however

Fortunately, however, there were some nobility who did happen to spot the vagabonds on the grass verges and began to invite them into their homes, or rather Stately Homes, to present their plays indoors. Plays such as *Gammer Gurton's Needle*, *Getting Gertie's Garter* and *Goethe's Faust.* Appallingly written, atrociously staged and yet somehow with that something *just a little bit different.*

Pounding

One can imagine the scene. A Tudor noble and his wife pounding down the M45 from Daventry to Kenilworth in their luxury coach and six.

'What will we do tonight?' asks the noble's wife, gloomily, 'after our massive nineteen-course dinner of peacock, plum duff, figgy pudding and flummery?'

'We could dance the evening away doing the gallimauphrey,' suggests the noble, somewhat halfheartedly.

'Not another evening danced away doing the gallimauphrey!' she replies.

'So what do you suggest we do?' he exclaims, reaching the end of his tether with electrifying rapidity.

And then suddenly – out of the blue, or rather the verge – *something catches her eye*.

Lay-by

It is a troop of vagabonds and Sturdy Beggars performing *Colin Clout Come Home Again* in a nearby lay-by. Valiantly competing with the roar of the traffic and the late November sleet lashing in off the as yet unenclosed Cheviots.

'That looks like something just a little bit different,' she exclaims. And leaning her head out of the luxury coach, she asks, 'Pray what art thou standing thus in paltry costume in a nearby lay-by disclaiming?'

Deep Surge

'We are a troop of Sturdy Beggars in the middle of *Colin Clout Come Home Again*, as it happens,' replies the Vagabond Manager. 'But if you wish we could go straight back to the start of Act One and start all over again at the drop of a hat.'

'But would not this oblige you to reset your props and so forth?' cries the lady noble, her eyes already aglitter.

'We have no props, seeing as we are but Sturdy Beggars doing a fringe show on a profit-share,' comes the reply. 'In other words, what props we have, we eat.'

Then suddenly the noble's wife feels a deep surge within her such as she has not felt since receiving her first pony.

*Fig. 3. Some Nobles suddenly spotting
some Sturdy Beggars by the roadside*

The birth of the theatre

'Then come with us!' she cries, 'to our big Tudor Hall and perform this *Colin Clout Come Home Again* before a roaring fire where at the moment are but two Irish wolfhounds asleep and my husband the Earl and myself who have little to say to one another any more, seeing as we married young and our children are grown and gone away.'

And so it was, the theatre was born.

THINGS TO DO:

1. Make a scale model of ONE of the following:
A gallimauphrey; the M45; Colin Clout; Daventry.

CHAPTER XX
SHAKESPEARE AND HIS PATRONS

'One man in his time has many Patrons.'

(Shakespeare)

Introduction

So, anyway, how was Shakespeare doing regarding Patrons at this time? In other words, had he discovered a Patron?

Or – to put it another way – had he managed to interest anybody in his corpus?

In other words, how long did he have to hang about on the M45 reciting bits from *As You Like It, Camelot* and *Mrs Warren's Profession* before a Patron finally spotted it?[1]

House of Lords

And the answer, of course, is not very long. In fact he had barely launched into the first half closer of *Henry VI, Part 3* when a massive luxury coach containing half of the House of Lords arrived, offering not only to build the Globe Theatre but also buy him a nineteen-course Elizabethan meal and a costume budget.

---

[1] His corpus.

Welkin

Four weeks later, Shakespeare had more Patrons than he knew what to do with. Hence the famous line:

'The welkin's vice-regent and sole dominator of
Navarre, my soul's earth's god, and body's
fost'ring Patron. Not a word of Costard yet'.

Which is one of the most bewildering lines ever written, but means more or less the same thing.

So, finally, what actually did Shakespeare do with his Patrons?

Point-to-Point

Basically, Shakespeare and his Patrons spent their days doing a number of things, namely, going to point-to-points, examining his corpus and designing the Globe Theatre, which was easier said than done, of course, because nobody had any idea what a theatre actually *looked* like. Least of all Shakespeare. Seeing as the only theatre they'd ever had, apart from the Sturdy Beggars on the motorway, were *Mystery Plays*, so named because it was a mystery anybody understood them, and *Miracle Plays*, because it was a miracle they ever got on in the first place.

Shakespeare and his Patrons

Leg Room

Hence it's hardly surprising the Bard had an enormous number of 'false starts', so to speak, before finally arriving at a design everyone could be happy with. Particularly, of course, the Patrons who wanted the best view, plenty of leg room and their own bar.

Conclusion

And finally – probably the most important question of all – who were Shakespeare's Patrons?

Unfortunately, once again, it is not possible to name Shakespeare's Patrons, seeing as there were so many of them, obviously. Hence the famous line:

'Call Warwick Patron and be penitent?'

The meaning of which, again, is almost entirely unclear but does put in a very cogent nutshell, in my opinion, the reason it is not actually possible to 'name the Patrons', so to speak.

So who were some of his Patrons?

On second thoughts, however, I do feel it might be handy for the reader to have a brief list of some of the Patrons who were Shakespeare's Patrons. Which is as follows, basically:

List of some of Shakespeare's Patrons

Charles II
David Garrick
Catherine the Great
Jane Seymour
Edward VII
Edward VIII
Mrs Simpson
Barbara Windsor
The Earl of Essex
David Essex
Adam Faith
Richard III
Florence Nightingale
Mrs Shusha Guppy
Martyn Lewis
The Early of Ronaldshay and the Hon. Mary Anne Denison-Pender
Pope Gregory VI
Martin Marprelate
The Bishop of Ipswich
Maurice of Nassau
The Laird of Atholl
Lord Montague of Beaulieu
Nelson Mandela
Tiny Rowland

St Thomas Aquinas
Placido Domingo
Princess Kyril of Bulgaria
The Countess of Lichfield
The Marchioness of Worcester
Raine Countess Spencer
Sophie Thynn
Ivana Trump
Beethoven
Mrs Didi Saunders
Viscount and Viscountess Scarsdale
Lord and Lady Brabazon of Tara
Philip II of Spain
Crown Prince Naruhito of Japan
Mr Chisholm Wallace
Archduchess Walburga von Habsburg
Miss Bumble Fleming
Miss Trini Woodall
Scott of the Antarctic
Dame Julian of Norwich
Miss Camilla Belloc Lowndes
The Smashing Pumpkins
Queen Anne-Marie of the Hellenes

The Duke of Somerset
Lambert Simnel
Alan Yentob
Leonardo da Vinci
Sting

Mr William Corsett
The Hon. John and Mrs Fermor-
  Hesketh
Miss Louisa Welby-Everard

THINGS TO DO:

1. Write an essay entitled EITHER 'Who would I patronise if I had the chance?' OR 'Who wouldn't I mind being patronised by, as it happens?'

2. Paraphrase the following in your own words: *Henry VI, Part 3*; Miss Camilla Belloc Lowndes; *Camelot*.

3. Write a five-act tragedy entitled EITHER *Ivana Trump* OR *Placido Domingo* OR *Alan Yentob*.

CHAPTER XXI

DID THE QUEEN MEET SHAKESPEARE?

'The carl spak oo thing.'

(Chaucer)

O NE of the questions that Shakespearean experts such as me get asked *pretty much all the time* is:

Did Shakespeare ever meet the Queen? Or, to put it another way, did the Queen ever meet Shakespeare? Certainly she did when he was a fashionable playwright in London. But I also believe – contrary to what is generally held – that Shakespeare also met the Queen on a number of other occasions previous to the famed occasion in 1678 when Shakespeare was first summonsed to Buckingham Palace to have Audience with the Queen following the success of his West End hit, *A Man For All Seasons.*

But how can I be so sure?

Well, as we know, in Shakespeare's teenage years the population of the UK was minuscule compared to today – owing to the Black Death, Lollards and male fertility decline due to tights. For this reason large urban centres, such as Stratford-upon-Avon, Historic Warwick and Hendon-on-Thames, were virtually empty.

In other words it wouldn't have been beyond the realms of possibility for the Queen and Shakespeare to have met by chance, so to speak, *seeing as there were so few people about.*

Let us imagine the scene.

A leafy glade beside the gurgling waters of an English brook. Suddenly a bare-faced stripling comes face to face with a mature redhead. Neither knowing who the other is, of course. Or rather, Shakespeare would probably have known who she was, I should imagine, owing to the four hundred bullock carts, two thousand four hundred pack horses, seven thousand nine hundred scullions and four thousand Scots Dragoons shuddering to a grinding halt behind her.

Scene: A leafy glade. A brook gurgles. Enter the QUEEN.

QUEEN. Ah.

SHAKESPEARE. Excuse me.

We hear the sound of bullock carts, scullions and Scots Dragoons shuddering and halting all the way back to Leamington Spa.

QUEEN. Who art thou? O saucy fellow?

SHAKESPEARE. A yeoman bold, my virgin Queen.

QUEEN. So where art thou from, oh yeoman bold?

SHAKESPEARE. From leafy Warwickshire, my lovelorn Liege.

QUEEN. Historic Warwick?

SHAKESPEARE. No, from Stratford.

QUEEN. Stratford?

SHAKESPEARE. Yea, my Monarch, from the Mid Land.

QUEEN. From the *Mid* Land?

SHAKESPEARE. Or rather, the Mid *Lands* as they be known.

QUEEN. The Mid *Lands*?

SHAKESPEARE. Yea, fair Vestal.

QUEEN. Then let them be known henceforth as the Mid *Lands* then. Or rather –

SHAKESPEARE. Yea, my spotless Liege.

QUEEN. The Midlands.

SHAKESPEARE. The Midlands?

QUEEN. Why not?

SHAKESPEARE. A marvellous idea, my regal Ruler.

QUEEN. Then the Midlands shall they be.

SHAKESPEARE. Very well.

QUEEN. So where are we now then, oh nimble fellow?

SHAKESPEARE. I'm not quite with you, my sanguine Sovereign?

QUEEN. Are we east or west or where precisely?

SHAKESPEARE. The West Midlands, oh faery Queen.

QUEEN. Then name we this the West Midlands.

SHAKESPEARE. So be it, my pristine Pontiff.

QUEEN. Right then. Anyway, I'd better get on with my progress.

SHAKESPEARE. Don't let me stand in your way.

QUEEN. Thank you. *(She laughs ruefully.)* Rather slow progress today, I'm afraid.

SHAKESPEARE *(laughing ruefully also)*. Huh!

Call this the idle jottings of a fanciful mind if you will, but I hope it possibly encourages the reader in my fascinating notion that William Shakespeare met Her Majesty Queen Elizabeth I prior to what was thought previous.

However, once the author of *Timon of Athens*, *Sleuth* and *Relative Values* had seen his name in lights, did the Queen, the Vestal Virgin of all England, ever, in fact, meet him again?

And the answer, of course, is of course she did.

The Queen (or the QEI as she became known) was always extremely keen to meet new faces in the public eye. In fact, the moment an up-and-coming face appeared, they were summonsed instantly to Buckingham Palace (or Balmoral or Crystal Palace or wherever the Royal Progress happened to have reached at the time) to have what was known as 'Audience with the Queen'.

So how, or rather where, did Queen Elizabeth I meet 'up-and-coming young Tudor faces' in the fourteenth century?

Well, we can safely say that it wasn't over lunch, seeing as lunch wasn't a meal people had in those days. So much so that there wasn't even a word for lunch in the Tudor Epoch. Comb through the *Complete Works of Shakespeare*, for example, and you will find not a single reference to the word 'lunch'. 'Lurch' yes, 'lump', 'lumpish', 'lumpfish', 'luggage', 'lust', 'lunes', 'lunatic' and 'lurking place', but – as I say – not a mention of the word 'lunch', 'mid-day meal' or even 'bar snack'.

Part of the Royal Progress

So did the Tudors have any breakfast then?

Yes, generally speaking, the Tudors would start their day with a very large breakfast consisting of tea, coffee, fruit juice, choice of cereals, fried egg, bacon, sausage, mushroom, tomato, toast and preserves, followed by a large syllabub.

And after that?

After that they had nothing at all until dinner, which was generally fifty-two courses and lasted nine hours. Consisting of such things as minced collops; Bismarck herring; Haddock Monte Carlo; plover in the hole; *Fourme d'Ambert* cheese in quiche Reine Claude; compôte of fricasséed Ptarmigan; and chicken drumsticks. For pudding, there was Swiss roll, Tyrolean hazelnut torte, morello cherry cheesecake and tutti-frutti ice-cream with orange foam sauce.

So was it at just such a dinner that the Queen and Shakespeare might have met and conversed, then?

Yes it was, in my opinion.

In fact, looking at all the available evidence it is my belief we can safely assume that Queen Elizabeth I – the Regina Dominatrix of the United Kingdom and all her Commonwealth – personally summonsed Shakespeare to dinner at Buckingham Palace and therefore met him and had much conversation with him and did know him also. Partly because he was the most famed person in all England, but also because the Queen was in fact a keen amateur playwright herself and clearly anxious to run a couple of ideas 'by him' so to speak. Or, as he himself put it, 'up his flagpole to see if anyone salutes' (*Measure for Measure* V; iv; 307). Mind you, she was a highly sensitive person and one could never be too careful. She ran a couple of ideas 'by' Sir Walter Raleigh, for instance, and look what happened to him. Not to mention Lady Jane Gray, Mary Queen of Scots, Louis XVI and Dr Crippen, all of whom spoke their mind just a little too freely in my opinion. Not to mention her opinion, obviously.

Once again, let us picture the scene:

Buckingham Palace. Day. Fifteenth Century. The distant sound of the Changing of the Guard. Enter QUEEN ELIZABETH I.

QUEEN ELIZABETH I. Who are we having audience with today, herald?

Enter HERALD.

HERALD. Will Shakespeare, your Highness.

QUEEN ELIZABETH I. Will Shakespeare what?

HERALD. Will Shakespeare the well-known Elizabethan playwright, your Highness.

QUEEN ELIZABETH I. Playwright, eh?

HERALD. Playwright, your Highness.

QUEEN ELIZABETH I. Then attend Will Shakespeare!

HERALD. Attend Will Shakespeare!

Enter WILL SHAKESPEARE.

QUEEN ELIZABETH I. Are you Will Shakespeare?

WILL SHAKESPEARE. I am, your Highness.

1   2   3

4. Shakespearean Acting 1: 'Doing the Turn'

QUEEN ELIZABETH I. What thinkst thou of my latest play?

WILL SHAKESPEARE. Fabulous, your Highness.

QUEEN ELIZABETH I. You're not just saying that?

WILL SHAKESPEARE. Absolutely not, my limpid Liege.

QUEEN ELIZABETH I. Then what thinkst thou of the line, 'Airley Beacon, Airley Beacon; oh! the pleasant sight to see'?

WILL SHAKESPEARE (*slight pause*). I love it.

QUEEN ELIZABETH I. 'Airley Beacon, Airley Beacon; Oh the pleasant sight to see.'

WILL SHAKESPEARE. Fabulous!

QUEEN ELIZABETH I. Dine with me tonight!

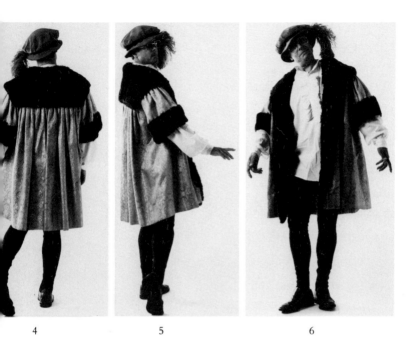

4   5   6

WILL SHAKESPEARE. What will we be having?

QUEEN ELIZABETH I. What will we be having?

WILL SHAKESPEARE. Just as a matter of interest.

QUEEN ELIZABETH I. We will be having minced collops; Bismarck
herring; Haddock Monte Carlo; plover in the hole; *Fourme
d'Ambert* cheese in quiche Reine Claude; compôte of fricasséed
Ptarmignon and chicken drumsticks.

WILL SHAKESPEARE. And for pudding?

QUEEN ELIZABETH I. Swiss roll, Tyrolean hazelnut torte, morello
cherry cheesecake and tutti-frutti ice-cream with orange foam
sauce.

WILL SHAKESPEARE. Fabulous!

QUEEN ELIZABETH I. It's something I rustled up earlier.

WILL SHAKESPEARE. Please allow me to accept your majesty's kind invite!

QUEEN ELIZABETH I *(coyly behind fan)*. But of course, my pretty nimble-witted fellow.

WILL SHAKESPEARE. Phew! That was a close one.

QUEEN ELIZABETH I. I beg your pardon?

WILL SHAKESPEARE. I said, 'But soft, what light through yonder window breaks.'

QUEEN ELIZABETH I. Herald?

HERALD. Yes, your Highness?

QUEEN ELIZABETH I. Lead us to the collops!

WILL SHAKESPEARE. The what?

QUEEN ELIZABETH I. To the collops!

HERALD. To the collops!

OTHER HERALDS *(off)*. To the collops!

Flourish. Exeunt QUEEN *and* HAROLD.

WILL SHAKESPEARE. To the collops!

Exeunt WILL SHAKESPEARE.

THINGS TO DO:

1. Meet the Queen.
2. Meet the Duke of Edinburgh.

CHAPTER XXII
DID OTHER FAMOUS PEOPLE OF HIS EPOCH ALSO MEET SHAKESPEARE?

'Feret haec aliquam tibi fama salutem.'
[Fame is nothing to a saluting ferret.]

(Virgil, *Aeneid*, Book 1, line 461)

ONE of the many fascinating questions I am often asked is, 'Did other famous people of his Epoch also meet Shakespeare?' And the answer, of course, is very much so.

In fact, Shakespeare knew so many famous people of his Epoch that it would take considerably more space than I have here, unfortunately, to detail the many in-depth meetings that would have almost certainly occurred.

Here, anyway, is a list of most, if not all, of the other famous people of Shakespeare's Epoch with a handy reference section to assist the student in spotting at a glance exactly which ones he met and – more important – how well he actually knew them.

FAMOUS PEOPLE OF THE EPOCH
(And which ones Shakespeare knew)

	Very well	Quite well	Nodding terms
Queen Elizabeth I	✓		
Sir Francis Drake	✓		
Marco Polo	✓		
Christopher Wren	✓		
Don Quixote	✓		
Genghis Khan	✓		
Beaumont and Fletcher	✓		
Leonardo da Vinci	✓		
Lady Jane Grey		✓	
Dorothy Perkins	✓		
Louis XIV	✓		
Sir Walter Raleigh	✓		
Galileo	✓		
Picasso	✓		
Mozart			✓

Thus it becomes immediately clear that not only did Shakespeare meet all of the other famous people of his Epoch but was certainly very good friends with most of them as well.

In fact, comparing the above list to Mozart's list, for instance (see facing page), we will see immediately how truly enormous was Shakespeare's popularity, particularly in comparison to Mozart's.

Genghis Khan

DID OTHER FAMOUS PEOPLE MEET SHAKESPEARE?

FAMOUS PEOPLE OF THE EPOCH
(And which ones Mozart knew)

	Very well	Quite well	Nodding terms
Queen Elizabeth I			✓
Marco Polo			✓
Joan of Arc			✓
Michelangelo			✓
Christopher Wren			✓
Genghis Khan		✓	
Inigo Jones			✓
Beaumont and Fletcher			✓
Chaucer			✓
Lady Jane Grey			✓
Sir Walter Raleigh			✓
Galileo			✓
Grace Darling	✓		
El Cid		✓	
William the Conqueror			✓
Shakespeare			✓

Finally, and in conclusion, while Shakespeare knew an enormous number of the many famous personages of his Epoch, he was always extremely unassuming and considerate to such people as the common-or-garden man in the street, pets and children, i.e. albeit he was famous he didn't brag about it to all and sundry all the time unlike some I could mention, without naming names obviously.

THINGS TO DO:

1. Meet a lot of famous personages of your Epoch.

CHAPTER XXIII
DID SHAKESPEARE TRAVEL TO ITALY
– AND IF SO, WHY?

'Scusi, a che ora parta il prossimo autobus per Firenze?'

(Leonardo da Vinci)

IT was during my researches into the last chapter that I came up with possibly one of the most intriguing theories ever put forward regarding the Bard and also, without wishing to blow my trumpet obviously, one of the most major anyone has ever had, in this field.

What struck me was basically as follows.

Something so blindingly obvious that it is hardly surprising nobody has yet spotted it.

How come nearly all of Shakespeare's plays are set in Italy?

Literally, *virtually every one of his plays* is either set *in Italy* or has something *astonishingly Italianate* about its title. *Two Gentlemen of Verona*, for instance, *Death in Venice*, *Three Coins in a Fountain*, *Roman Holiday*, *Timon of Athens*. The list is endless.

In other words, what I'm asking is this:

How come he knew all about Italy all of a sudden?

Had he simply read about it? We certainly know he *could* read. Hence the well-known line:

> 'wide unclasp the tables of their thoughts to every ticklish reader and set them down for sluttish spoils and daughters of the game'.

But it doesn't explain how he could have gained his astounding background knowledge, such as his extraordinarily expert grasp of authentic names, like Juliet, for instance, or Placido Domingo.[1]

In other words, is it possible that Shakespeare – Bard of all the Avons – actually *travelled to Italy*?

We certainly know there was a rudimentary travel industry. Not as advanced as ours, maybe, but nevertheless most High Streets – plague-ridden and running with sewage as they were – did sport a couple of rudimentary Cooks and at least one Hogg Robinson amongst the whipping posts and oyster bars of Tudor London.

Leaning Tower of Pisa

So – if Shakespeare did travel to Italy – *why did he go?*

Was it simply for 'research purposes', or was there in fact a *darker reason*?

In other words, and not to beat about the bush, was Shakespeare, in fact, a spy?

And the definitive answer to this fascinating, if controversial, query is, in my opinion, almost definitely yes. Not all the time, obviously (otherwise how could he have written thirty-seven plays, let alone trekked to Tibet!!), but nevertheless on a fairly regular basis. And, although this has not, as yet, been actually proved, it is my personal belief that it is in fact *all too true*.

So what is my evidence for such a claim?

Basically, I base my claim for such a shocking claim on ONE

[1] Or Dame Kiri Te Kanawa, as he is also known.

SIMPLE BUT INCONTROVERTIBLE SURMISE, which is basically as follows:

That Shakespeare's agent was more than what he claimed to be, i.e. *an agent*.

In fact, quite a bit more!

In fact that Shakespeare's agent (unnameable, for legal reasons, obviously) wasn't in fact an agent at all, but a SECRET agent – in the direct employ of Sir Francis Walsingham himself, and running a number of playwright/spies out of his basement office at:

Peter Frasere and Dunloppe Associates

No 19, Greek Street,

Cheapskate

Including Beaumont and Fletcher, Huntley and Palmer, Jonson and Johnson, Lilley and Skinner and, of course, Ralph Roister-Doister. The same men, in other words, who Shakespeare had 'roomed with' so long ago in Morecambe, but whose theatrical activities were clearly A COVER for their work for British Intelligence.

Dorothy Perkins

This of course immediately explains a number of 'Shakespearean mysteries' that have baffled experts for centuries. Namely:

a) The reason the words *spy* and *agent* appear in the Bard's Works with such astonishing regularity:

'He *spying* her, bounced in'

for instance, or even more significantly:

'Night's black *agents* to their preys do rouse'

which is clearly an explicit reference to one's 'theatrical agent', but ALSO – on closer analysis – a veiled reference to the 'secret agent', which, as we now know, was a very common agent to be and far more common than all the other kinds of agents of the time, such as insurance agents, travel agents or estate agents, for example.[1]

b) The reason why the Spanish Armada failed in 1588 – which was entirely due to the intelligence as to its whereabouts gleaned by Shakespeare and his team of under-cover playwrighting espionage experts.

Conclusion

In other words, we can safely say if it hadn't been for them and particularly the Immortal Swan himself, the UK might have been *a very different place indeed*, i.e. if the Armada had succeeded, here are some of the things ordinary English folk might today take as *totally normal daily occurrences*:

1. Eating paella;
2. Going to endless bullfights;
3. Hosting the 1992 Olympic Games.

The End of the Spanish Armada

THINGS TO DO:

1. Write short notes on three of the following:
Greek Street; Hogg Robinson; the English Channel; Sluttish spoils; Placido Domingo; Huntley and Palmer; Sewage; Ralph Roister-Doister.

2. Compose a letter as if to ONE of the following:
A Tudor Estate Agent; A Tudor Travel Agent; A Tudor Secret Agent (use invisible ink). **N.B.** Do *not* send it, obviously (particularly to the Secret Agent).

---

[1] This becomes immediately clear, of course, when one notes that the word 'insurance' *never* appears in any of Shakespeare's works and 'estate agent' only a couple of times at the end of *Cymbeline*.

CHAPTER XXIV
THE MIDDLE YEARS
DAYS OF HOPE

'Mid age and wrinkled eld.'

(Act V:ii:612, *Troilism and Cressida*)

AFTER the Early Years came the Middle Years. Probably, it is now believed, as a result of meeting Thomas Middleton, moving to Middlesex and writing *Middlemarch*. The value of Shakespeare's Middle Years has sometimes been questioned, but nevertheless, without the Middle Years, Shakespeare could never have moved on to the Final Years. Which, of course, came later.

And then suddenly – just as his life appeared to be dipping into the gloom of his final twilight – something extraordinary occurred. Something he never believed possible.

The builders finally finished the Globe Theatre.

Within seconds, and without even finishing his pudding, Shakespeare grasped his quill and took the first barge to Bankside.

Arriving moments later, he watched them put the finishing touches to the central heating or 'global warming' system before finally realising that at last he'd begun his last and probably greatest years: The Globe Years. Immortalised of course in some of his greatest plays which are of course too numerous to mention at this juncture.

5. Shakespearean Fights and Combat 1:
'On Guard!'

Conclusion

For a full appreciation of Shakespeare's famed Globe Years and what he did with them, let us now turn to the ensuing chapter, 'Shakespeare's Famed Globe Years – and What He Did With Them'.

THINGS TO DO:

1. Write short notes on at least ONE of the following: Globoid; globose; glob; global artichoke; haemoglobin; Harlem Globetrotters.

CHAPTER XXV

SHAKESPEARE'S FAMED GLOBE YEARS –
AND WHAT HE DID WITH THEM

'Oh that this too, too wooden globe would melt!'

(Shakespeare)

AN essential prerequisite of examining William Shakespeare, of course, is to very much 'get to know' the Globe Theatre. In fact, to become thoroughly *'au fait'* with this fascinating building is an absolute imperative for the Shakespearean student.

So where should one begin?

In my opinion, one should always begin with the same thing when one examines a theatre, and the Globe is certainly no exception.

In other words, one should always begin *with the scenery*.

So what is the scenery?

The scenery and what is it?

The scenery is basically probably the most important single aspect of any play. In other words, without the scenery what do you have? Answer: nothing.

91

No scenery

And that is one thing an audience just won't take. They'll take a lot, but one thing they won't take is *no scenery*.

Relentless Heat

Audiences pay a *great deal* for a good seat at the theatre. Many of whom are ordinary working people such as welders, miners and postmen and so forth. Men and women who spend hours of every day welding rivets, hacking at the coal seam and delivering letters in the relentless heat.

'*If we give them nothing else,*' as Sir Peter Brook said to me not so long ago, '*the least we can do is give them a good set.*'

And Shakespeare of course – a man who knew virtually everything there was to know about work – would have been the *very first to agree*.

Or would he?

Disturbing Feature

Because, when one examines the Elizabethan theatre – or Globe obviously – via the numerous etchings and ground plans of the time, it isn't long before one notices a very disturbing feature indeed, which is:

THERE IS ABSOLUTELY NO SCENERY WHATSO-EVER.

A couple of chairs possibly, a bit of old curtain at the back. And that's basically it.

Almost Incredible

So why is this? Or rather, was this?

Why – when we know Shakespeare was very much a 'scenery man' and extremely sympathetic to the miners and postmen and so forth – did he in fact have *no scenery whatsoever*?

For the almost incredible answer to this fascinating conundrum, let us now turn to the ensuing chapter, 'Shakespeare and the Scenery Problem: A Riddle Solved'.

THINGS TO DO:

1. Write a tragedy about EITHER a welder OR a postman in the style of EITHER *Much Ado About Nothing* OR *The Postman Always Rings Twice* OR *The Postman Occasionally Knocks Once* OR *The Postman Pops in From Time to Time.*

Shakespeare meets the Queen

CHAPTER XXVI
SHAKESPEARE AND THE SCENERY PROBLEM
A RIDDLE SOLVED

'The scenery is now transported to Southampton.'

(Shakespeare)

So why – in short – did Shakespeare have no scenery, basically? Was it that he didn't want it?

No, I can safely say that Shakespeare desperately wanted scenery. In fact he wanted scenery more than he could say.

So why didn't he have any scenery then?

For one simple and painful reason. Namely, the Groundlings.

The Groundlings?

Yes, and, more to the point, the Problem with the Groundlings.

So what was the Groundlings and, more to the point, the Problem with the Groundlings then?

The Groundlings, as any Shakespeare expert will tell you, was basically the great unwieldy surging tide of man, the mighty jostling hubbub of the common weal of England, upon whose toiling backs this mighty realm was forged and in whose footsteps we are surely proud to stand. Those same men and women who stood at Agincourt and Bannockburn, who fought the Great Fire of London and built St Paul's Cathedral.

So what was the problem then, as such?

The problem was that, although they was indeed the unwieldy mighty backbone of all England, proud navigators of our sea-encompassed vessel and surging forebears of this mighty island heritage and royal womb of teeming kings, the Groundlings was entirely illiterate and therefore had absolutely no idea what was going on when they came to the theatre.

Which would have been fine if they had kept quiet, presumably.

Exactly. Modern audiences watching Shakespeare have no idea what's going on either, but they don't make a song and dance about it. They simply sit there silently and politely not understanding a single word.

You can say that again.

Unfortunately, however, this was not the case with the Tudor Groundlings who thronged relentlessly into the stalls night after night only to spend the entire performance heckling, picking each other's pockets and chucking orange peel at the actors.

In other words, complete and utter mayhem?

It certainly was! In fact, Shakespeare experts agree that why the Groundlings ever came to the theatre in the first place – to see what are, after all, some of the longest and most baffling plays ever written – is a complete and utter mystery. A mystery on a par, in fact, with some of the greatest mysteries of all time, such as what happened to the Marie Celeste.

Is there a Yeti?

Quite. However, after a massive amount of in-depth research in both London, Stratford and numerous other places as well, I believe I am now in a position to offer an astonishing solution to BOTH mysteries. Namely, the Groundlings' mysterious devotion to William Shakespeare *and* the bizarre disappearance of all of his scenery. And not only that. I also intend to prove that the two mysteries are *indissolubly connected*!

Fascinating!

I hope so. The Groundlings, being the surging, jostling hubbub of the common weal of all England, not to mention the impregnable forebears of our mighty island fortress, were also, of course, phenomenally poor. So that when they surged down Shaftesbury Avenue into the Globe Theatre for the first time and saw an entire Tudor Baronial Hall staring them in the face, complete with chandeliers, cut-glass goblets, hand-woven tapestries and Fabergé eggs all over the place, it's hardly surprising that, by the first interval, the entire thing had completely vanished.

Good Lord! The Groundlings, in other words, had stolen it, basically?

Yes. And thus began probably the worst problem there was for theatre managements of the day. Certainly, worse, in many respects, than many of the other well-known theatre problems they had to face as well.

So were there many other well-known theatre problems of the day, then, while we're on the subject?

Fig. 3. The Yeti

Yes, there certainly were.

Such as what, for example?

Other well-known theatre problems of the time included: below par line-learning; lack of adequate roofing facilities; toxic prop fatalities; the critics rioting for interval drinks; arson; and appalling upstaging. Some of which will be dealt with in considerable detail in later chapters and some of which, owing to the panoramic yet necessarily comprehensive scale of this work, unfortunately won't. But, anyway, back to the Groundlings and the nicking of the scenery problem.

So what actually happened when the Groundlings nicked all the scenery then?

Well, basically, what actually happened was the actors would return after the interval for Act II only to find that whole sets that had been standing moments before – staircases, French windows, fitted carpets, siege engines and so forth – had completely and utterly disappeared.

So the Groundlings had just upped and offed with the lot, basically?

Well, not *all* the Groundlings, obviously.

Not all *the Groundlings?*

No. In fact, I can safely say that *most* Groundlings had absolutely no interest in scenery-nicking whatsoever. In point of fact, they did their utmost to enjoy the play. Often bringing with them their own texts which they laboriously and pedantically followed throughout the performance.[1]

So who was it then who done the nicking?

I am of course referring to the criminal element of Tudor London.

Good heavens.

Or rather Underground.

The London Underground, in other words?

Precisely. Or cutpurses, jades and bawdy baskets.

So how did they do it, actually?

Nick all the scenery?

Yes.

Well, let me put it this way. The cutpurses and jades and so forth became so astonishingly adept at scene-shifting, as it became known, that it was in fact possible, while an audience was rioting for interval drinks in the bar and the actors had their feet up in the green

---

[1] These were, of course, the famed Methuen Playtexts – introduced by the current Lord Methuen's ancestor, Earl Methuen of Nottingham, and penned by hand onto expensive vellum by the Earl's editorial staff.

Needless to say, early Methuen Playtexts, although now recognised as a boon to playgoers throughout the world, were something of a mixed blessing in the early days of the Globe, given the fact that basic Groundling literacy skills left a little to be desired. In fact, it must have been a deeply nerve-racking experience for the young Tudor actor just 'off the book' to find four or five hundred mead-swilling illiterate Groundlings chanting slavishly along in the background of each scene.

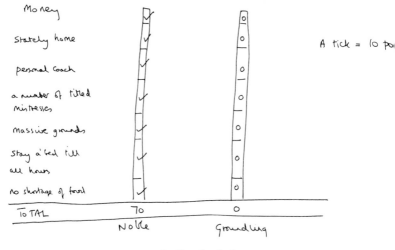

Money

Stately home

personal coach

a number of titled mistresses

massive grounds

Stay a'bed till all hours

no shortage of food

TOTAL — Noble: 70 — Groundling: 0

A tick = 10 po

Fig. 2. Graph of advantages
of being a Noble as opposed to a Groundling

room, for an entire set for *Antony and Cleopatra*, for example, to be dismantled, melted down, boxed up and – via the expertise of a million little nifty cutpurse fingers – on its way through the plague-infested London Underground of Tudor England to its final destination amongst the ruthless *Mafiosi* and black marketeers of Tudor Europe before the fanfare sounded for Act II.

Good Lord.

In fact, as demand grew for 'hot scenery', the cutpurses became more and more audacious in their methods. One of the most daring, not to say flagrant, was having a young jade or bawdy basket suddenly running into the theatre halfway through a particularly poignant love scene and shouting, 'Plague! Plague!'

Within seconds, the theatre was empty and actors, usherettes and audience running pell-mell for Trafalgar Square and the well-known non-plague areas, such as Knightsbridge, Sloane Square and Cadogan Gardens.

So could it be said that as a result the Globe Management felt somewhat 'jaded'?

It certainly could!

I'm not surprised. So finally are there any further aspects of the Globe that need looking at?

Yes, there are one or two that need rather urgent attention as soon as possible.

So when shall we be looking at these, then?

In the next chapter, entitled 'The Globe Theatre: Further Aspects of the Globe'.

Not a moment too soon, in other words!

Exactly!

THINGS TO DO:

1. Paint a portrait of at least THREE of the following:
   a) Antony and Cleopatra; b) A Yeti; c) Cadogan Gardens.

2. Draw a map of the London Underground.

*Audience and usherettes
during the Plague*

CHAPTER XXVII
THE GLOBE THEATRE:
FURTHER ASPECTS OF THE GLOBE

'Her breasts like ivory globes;
a pair of maiden worlds
unconquered.'

(Shakespeare)

'Oh what a lovely Globe!'

(Shakespeare)

SO in order to examine the further aspects of the Globe that urgently need looking at, at this juncture, let us ask the following queries, which are as follows:

1. Did they have anything else in the Globe?
Yes, they also had the 'backstage area', which nobody really knows a great deal about, apart from the fact that it was virtually the same as it is today. In other words, readers 'in the business' won't want to hear about it all over again and more 'run-of-the-mill' readers who *aren't*, won't understand anyway.

But very briefly – as we've still got a lot to get through – it was just simply things like dressing rooms, corridors, wardrobe, admin block, toilet facilities, workshops and lighting desk etc.[1] In other words, nothing to get excited about.

2. So finally was there any Further Aspects of the Globe?

Yes, there was one which must be examined before we continue and is probably the most crucial Aspect of the Globe, in many respects.

It is, of course, the famed intimacy between actor and audience.

Queen Elizabeth I

3. So what generally speaking was the famed intimacy between actor and audience, basically?

The famed intimacy between actor and audience was what existed between actor and audience throughout Tudor England and was, more to the point, essential to make the plays work. In other words, without it, the plays generally didn't.

In fact, it was up to player and public to strike up an intimate rapport *as quickly as possible*[2] to make the evening a resounding success.

As Hamlet himself says in his famed speech to the old queen: 'Speak the speech, I pray you trippingly on the tongue and strike up an *intimate rapport with the public*[3] as quickly as possible.'

Fascinatingly, in fact, throughout the *Complete Works*, many characters harp on about exactly the same thing.

---

[1] Or lighting 'box' as it was more popularly known. Although, as lighting hadn't been invented yet, nobody quite knew what to do with it so generally it was just an empty room. In fact one of the great dilemmas of the Elizabethan theatre was 'what to do with the lighting box'. A dilemma that was never satisfactorily solved.
[2] My italics.
[3] Hamlet's italics.

Here, for instance, are Banquo and Macbeth on the foul heath. (Rendered into the modern idiom by myself for ease of comprehension by the contemporary audience):

Scene: A foul heath. Enter MACBETH *and* BANQUO.

MAC. So foul and fair a day I have not seen.

BAN. Nor have I. In fact, it's the foulest day I've ever seen.

MAC. Exactly.

>MAC *starts.*

BAN. Why start you, my Scottish thane?

MAC. At the name of Duncan!

BAN. Duncan?

MAC. Aggh!

BAN. But why, my laird?

MAC. It's been crossing my mind to murder him. As it has also my wife's, as it happens.

BAN. Lady Macbeth?

MAC. Yes.

BAN. That's ironic.

MAC. Just what I thought.

BAN. But you must not, my goodly liege. For he is a marvellous king.

MAC. He is, I know!!

BAN. And not only that. He is much loved by all and sundry. For he has the −

>MACBETH *starts again.*

MAC. Ah! Say it not!!

BAN. But I must, my highland henchman!

MAC. Go on then!

BAN. – Knack of striking up an instant rapport with the public.

MAC. Agh!! How I wish I had that knack!

BAN. Don't we all, my kilted captain?

MAC. Yea, a thousand times!

BAN. But that's no reason to murder him.

MAC. Absolutely.

BAN. Anyway, best be on our way.

They hover through the fog and filthy air. For a moment neither speaketh.

MAC. Not a word to the wife, eh?

BAN. About what, my plotting princeling?

MAC. My momentary show of weakness.

BAN. *(tapping the side of his nose)* Not a chuff or martlet, my thieving thane.

MAC. Marvellous.

Exeunt through fog.

Which I think makes my point *in a nutshell*, in my opinion.

*A scene from Shakespeare's
well-known Scottish tragic play*

4. Finally, were there ever problems regarding intimacy between actor and audience?

Yes, I'm afraid that sometimes there was too much intimacy, if you get my meaning.

In fact, plays were often held up, sometimes for several minutes, while members of the Company went missing – often to be discovered exploring various forms of actor–audience intimacy with selected members of the audience in a number of private backstage locations, such as the dressing rooms etc.

Many examples, of course, can be cited of 'over-enthusiastic intimacy exploration', as it was popularly termed. Particularly during some of Shakespeare's 'Problem' or 'Deviant' plays, such as *Troilism and Cressida* or *As You Like It*. One of the most famous occurred at the end of *The Winter's Tale* when the entire Bohemian Court was awaiting the famous moment when the statue of Hermione Gingold suddenly comes to life, bursts into a Hungarian Rhapsody and thereby 'saves the day'.

On this occasion, however, the curtains swept back to reveal nothing but an empty plinth, seeing as Miss Gingold – played by Sir Francis Burbridge whose actor–audience explorations were legion – was up in the empty lighting box exploring various upper-class lady fops, a couple of bawdy baskets and the critic from the *Stratford Advertiser*.[1]

The other actors, of course, were used to this kind of thing and, in any case, were probably backstage with various members of the audience themselves. For this reason, understudies were always standing by, ready to rush on at a moment's notice. Although, as like as not, they probably weren't, seeing as they were probably at it as well, seeing as the life of an understudy is a lonely one and who's to blame them?

5. So what, if any, was the solution?

Not surprisingly, the Globe was in a state of bedlam and a few days later, as a direct result of Shakespeare's intimacy problem, the Civil War (or American Civil War[2] as it was also known) exploded across Europe and closed all London's theatres until they reopened in 1953 with *The Lady's Not for Burning* at the Donmar Warehouse.

---

[1] Names withheld for legal reasons.
[2] Or Thirty Years War.

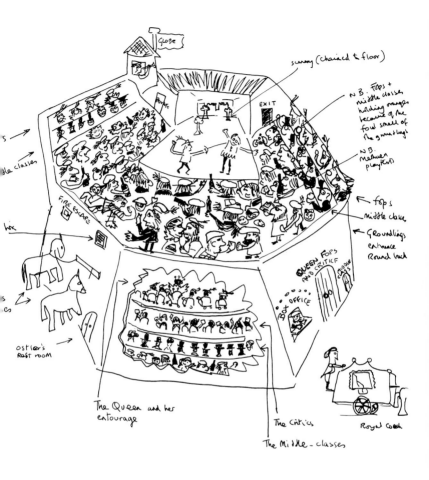

*The Globe Theatre
as it would have been
(artist's reconstruction)*

6. But how did Shakespeare actually write his plays at this time?

In other words, how did he go about it and what did he do when he did?

To answer this controversial question let us now turn to the following revealing chapter, 'How Shakespeare Wrote His Plays', and see how he did it, in my opinion.

THINGS TO DO:

1. Compose a sixteen-part motet on ONE of the following: Methuen Playtexts; admin. blocks; the Donmar Warehouse.

2. Write an up-to-the-minute novel entitled *The Bard and the Bawdy Basket*.

CHAPTER XXVIII
HOW SHAKESPEARE WROTE HIS PLAYS
or
THE PROBLEM WITH THE FOUL PAPERS

*'Though life's valley be a vale of tears
A brighter scene beyond that vale appears.*

(Mrs O. W. Holmes)

How Big?

Before embarking upon a new play, the very first thing the Bard had to do was decide how big to make it, i.e. whether to make it a Quarto, a First Folio, a Malvolio, a Bad Quarto or a Variorum Edition.

Unfortunately, however, seeing as we have no idea what these terms refer to, we must now move on to the second stage which is, of course, 'Penning the Work itself'.

An unpleasant discovery

Which brings me to an unpleasant discovery I have recently made concerning this fascinating topic, namely that what Shakespeare wrote his plays actually *on* was apparently called his 'Foul Papers'.

107

6. *Juliet Stevenson*

Which is probably one of the most unsavoury things I've yet come across whilst engaged upon the present volume.

So why were they so foul?

Needless to say, nobody is entirely certain exactly why the 'foul papers' were so foul or, indeed, in such a state, but a number of major solutions have been put forward. Such as:

a) *Groundling spittle.* Seeing as we know that the Groundlings spat a lot during the performance of Shakespearean plays, there is every reason to believe that they also spat a lot *whilst he was actually writing them*, i.e. by putting their heads through the open lattice-work windows and spitting on the text whilst it was still being penned. Not while he was there, hopefully, but while he was out of the room for a few moments, making a fennel salad or keeping urchins off his topiary.

b) *'Sack' soilage.* 'Sack' of course was an early or rudimentary form of ale or 'light ale' and much drunk at the time, particularly by tipplers, topers, tosspots and writers. With regard to the latter, 'soilage' or 'spillage' from sack was prevalent during most phases of the writing process, particularly during 'deadline stress' as it was known. Shakespeare, of course, was not a heavy drinker but probably did quaff quite a bit when he couldn't get a certain bit right or when he was being hounded by his publisher, Sir William Caxton, an early ancestor of Lord Methuen (see Appendix 3, 'The Publishing Dynasties of Britain at the Time of Shakespeare').

Anyway, whatever the reason, it makes it doubly miraculous that Shakespeare's plays ever got published at all, let alone performed, and certainly explains why much of him is so hard to make head nor tail of most of the time.

So is this, in fact, why so much of him appears virtually meaningless?

Yes it is, as it happens.

Due to all the Groundling spittle and sack soilage?

Exactly.

Good Lord! So is that the only reason why the Bard is hard to make head nor tail of then?

Yes, besides a number of other reasons why the Bard is hard to make head nor tail of as well, as a matter of interest.

So what might they be when they're at home?

For a full examination of all the other reasons why the Bard is impossible to make head nor tail of, the reader should turn immediately to the following chapter, 'Understanding Shakespeare'.

THINGS TO DO:

1. Describe in your own words why you think Shakespeare wrote at least THREE of the following:
'Pillicock sat on pillicock hill.'
'The Senoys are by th'ears.'
'Here ye lie baiting of bombards.'

CHAPTER XXIX
UNDERSTANDING SHAKESPEARE
A CRITICAL ANALYSIS

'And for to se, and eek for to be seye.'

(Chaucer)

Introduction

So what are some of the other reasons why the Bard is impossible to make head nor tail of or, to put it another way, doesn't make much sense?

Best Known to Himself

In my opinion, the reasons are quite simple and are as follows: *because he actually doesn't*. In other words, we should all stop losing sleep over trying to make sense of what was – for a number of reasons best known to himself – actually nothing but *complete and utter nonsense in the first place*.

What to make of it?

For instance, what are we supposed to make of a line, such as:

'What, is there none of Pygmalion's images newly-made woman to be had now for putting the hand in the pocket and extracting it clutch'd? What reply? Ha? What says't thou, Trot?'

In other words, does it actually mean anything or is it just a load of complete nonsense?

Nonsense
And the answer, I believe, is complete and utter nonsense.

Doing us all a favour
In fact Sir William Caxton would have been doing us all a favour, in my opinion, if he'd been a bit more ruthless in the first place and simply cut it out. In fact cut out all the bits in Shakespeare that *don't actually make sense*.

A slight problem
A slight problem, of course, would be found in the fact that some plays might be somewhat reduced in length. *All's Well That Ends Well*, for instance, would last approximately three and a half minutes, while plays such as *Henry VI, Part 3* and *Pericles*, a mere thirty seconds.

But at least we could make head nor tail of them.

Something to be grateful for
And even though they weren't exactly what the Bard wrote, they would be something, I believe, which we could all be grateful for. Something, in other words, which could speak to all peoples throughout the globe.

Bard
So let us look at an example of 'Shakespeare without the nonsense' to prove – I hope once and for all – that the Bard IS ALIVE TODAY AND FOR ALL TIME.

THE TRAGEDY OF PERICLES, PRINCE OF TYRE

Dramatis Personae

PERICLES, PRINCE OF TYRE
ANTIOCHUS, KING OF ANTIOCH
FOLLOWERS
DAUGHTER OF ANTIOCHUS
LORD CERIMON

A scene from Pericles

Enter ANTIOCHUS, PERICLES *and* FOLLOWERS.

ANT. Young Prince of Tyre, you have at large received
  The danger of the task you undertake.

PER. I have, Antiochus, and with a soul
  Embold'ned with the glory of her praise,
  Think death no hazard in this enterprise.

ANT. All right then.[1]

Exeunt. Music.

Enter again ANTIOCHUS, PERICLES *and* FOLLOWERS *and the*
DAUGHTER OF ANTIOCHUS *and* LORD CERIMON.

PER. After numerous and bold adventures more than can be told of
  here.
  Our son and daughter shall in Tyrus reign.
  Lord Cerimon, we do our longing stay
  To hear the rest untold. Sir, lead's the way.

CER. All right then.'[2]

Exeunt.

FINIS

---

[1] In fact this line is not strictly Shakespeare but one inserted by myself to add some
  much needed 'impetus' to the scene.
[2] See note 1.

SHAKESPEARE: THE TRUTH

THINGS TO DO:

1. Rewrite THREE of the following well-known Shakespearean plays with all the nonsense removed: *Hamlet*; *King Lear*; *Julius Caesar*; *Merchant of Venice*; *Henry IV, Part 2*; *Twice Around the Garden*.

2. Explain the following well-known words: 'Trot'; 'variorum edition'; 'Pericles'; 'tosspot'.

3. Make a paper then foul it.

CHAPTER XXX
THE DARK LADY OF THE SONNETS:
WHO WAS SHE?

'I have no idea.'

(Anon.)

MEANWHILE one of the most fascinating mysteries in the *Complete Life and Works of William Shakespeare* was, of course, The Dark Lady Of The Sonnets.

In other words, who on earth was she? Which in itself begs a number of further essential questions, namely why was she dark? Was she really a lady? And, if so, why the sonnets? Which aren't exactly Shakespeare at the peak of his corpus, if you get my meaning, and as I'm sure he'd be the first to admit.[1]

Not to be sniffed at

In other words, why not the Tragedies? Or the Comedies? Or even the Problem Plays? One could understand someone wanting to be

---

[1] Owing to various complex time contingencies and so forth, I have unfortunately not had the pleasure of reading Shakespeare's Sonnets in their entirety. Those, or rather the one, I did manage to get through did, however, succeed in giving me 'a flavour' so to speak of the overall general Sonnet situation. Convincing me, as I say, that they are not really all they're cracked up to be and are probably best avoided.

the Dark Lady of the Problem Plays, for example. That, surely, would be a role not to be sniffed at. In other words, imagine the man who penned 'aroint, aroint, thou contentious worm' suddenly coming out from behind a pillar and saying 'Excuse me, would you care to be the Dark Lady of the Problem Plays, by any chance?' I would be very surprised if most people's response wasn't a very clear 'Yes please!'

Lukewarm

If, on the other hand, however, the Immortal Swan came out from behind a half-timbered pillar and said 'I'm afraid Problem Plays are gone but how about the Sonnets?', I can't imagine the response being overly enthusiastic, to be honest. In fact, extremely lukewarm is probably a more likely reaction.

No nearer

But still we are no nearer answering the tantalising question which of course is who on earth was the Dark Lady of the Sonnets? And was she in fact a lady at all?

Patently absurd

Well, first of all, we can clear up the second half of this question right away, I'm happy to say, which is that any idea that the Dark Lady of the Sonnets wasn't in fact a lady is quite obviously patently absurd. Various suggestions have been put forward that the Dark Lady of the Sonnets was in fact a number of well-known Dukes or Earls, including the Duke of Bedford, the Earl of Essex, the Duke of Earl, the Marquis of Bath, Mr W.H. who was, in fact, the Duchess of Windsor, and Anne Princess of Bohemia. In other words, it was a confusing situation and a mistake anyone could have made.

Ambisexual foreparts

It was also Elizabethan England, don't forget, which wasn't exactly renowned for its lack of sexual ambiguity. In fact it was such an ambiguous time that most people spent much of their lives wandering through various ornamental mazes desperately trying to establish exactly what sex they were. Indeed, many was the desperately ambiguous person to be found sobbing beneath a particularly ornate piece of Elizabethan topiary, over a hopeless confusion of earrings, tights, codpieces, kirtles and ambisexual foreparts. But we digress into areas that are not the brief of this mighty volume.

Beaver

What I'm saying is basically this, why on earth would William Shakespeare, the Bard-upon-Avon, the man who wrote 'they are oft tarr'd over with the surgery of sheep' and 'I'll put my silver beard in a gold beaver and in my vambrace put my withered brawns', dedicate all his Sonnets to the Dark Lady of the Sonnets if what he meant was the Dark Gentleman of the Sonnets?

Feet

In other words, even if the rest of Elizabethan England walked around with its feet in both camps, *Shakespeare certainly didn't*. He knew exactly which camp his feet were in, thank you very much. That's where they were and that's where they stayed.

Conclusion

And thus it is possible to prove conclusively that the Dark Lady of the Sonnets – if she existed at all – was definitely 'every inch a lady'.

And so – finally – we are left with the burning question.

Namely, who on earth was she?

The Dark Lady?

Who on earth was she?

In other words who was the mysteriously dark lady who haunted the Bard throughout his days, despite the fact that he was a deeply happily married man?

Sold Out

Europe was in uproar. The Sonnets, only recently on the bookstalls, had sold out within minutes and it was only a matter of hours before dark ladies of every shape, size and description were thronging the streets of Stratford desperate to discover which of them was in fact 'the lucky lady'. Or rather 'the Dark Lady', obviously.

Rumours were rife, names furiously mooted, but still nobody knew.

The only problem being: *neither did Shakespeare.*

Mystery Solved

In fact, *I am now in a position to reveal* what has long been suspected, but never before proved. And is basically this:

The reason he wrote:

> Oh! What a lovely creature
> In your lovely dress and bonnet
> Why I could nearly eat yer
> Dark Lady Of The Sonnets.

> (Sonnet CXVIII)

and not something more autobiographical, such as:

> Our liaison is quite something,
> By the second it gets steamier
> Oh! You get my heart a pumpin'
> Oh! Princess of Bohemia!

was not because he was keeping anything secret or had anything at all to be ashamed of, but because *he himself had absolutely no idea who she was.*

Conclusion

And so, having solved this fascinating and tantalising mystery 'half as timeless as time itself', let us approach the Swan of Avon one final time as he himself approaches his own Swan Song in a manner of speaking.

THE DARK LADY OF THE SONNETS

THINGS TO DO:

1. Paint a vast public mural in your local town centre entitled 'A Foot in Both Camps'.

2. Write a Sonnet including the following words: 'bookstalls'; 'Essex'; 'marriage guidance'; 'various'; 'beaver'; 'Bath'; 'sonnet'; 'brawns'; 'the Dark Lady of the Sonnets'.

CHAPTER XXXI
THE DEATH OF SHAKESPEARE

'Oh death where is thy sting-a-ling-a-ling?'

(Milton)

AND then it was that Shakespeare, quite unexpectedly, grew extraordinarily old. He could never tell the exact moment or the precise location, but suddenly, one morning, as he walked down Pudding Lane, he knew.

The following day, the doorbell rang and an old man was at the door.

'Yes?' said Will, his eyesight suddenly failing, 'and who might you be?'

'Old Time the clock-setter,' replied the old man, 'that bald sexton, Time.'

'Thank you,' said Will, 'I'll just pop into the theatre to make a small announcement.'

Unfortunately, nobody was at the theatre, seeing as they was all out watching the boat race, so Shakespeare said:

> Our revels now are ended. These are actors,
> As I foretold you, were all spirits and
> Are melted into air, into thin air

to no one in particular, then went home for his toothbrush and a change of tights and, finding none of his wives to say goodbye to, walked to Victoria and caught the first coach home.

Seventeen hours later, Shakespeare suddenly cried to the coachman, 'I recognise this bridge.' And alighting with nothing but his holdall, he spied through the early swirling mist of dawn a figure standing still as stone.

'How's the daub and wattle?' he asked, after a dreadful silence.

'Fine,' she replied.

'And the twins?'

'One is dead and the other married a gynaecologist.'

'And the grim-faced baby?'

'Moved to Newcastle.'

'Everything else all right?'

'Your sister married a hatter.'

'I thought I might come home now.'

'Fair enough.'

'And buy various properties and so forth and sit in the garden of our twilight years.'

'It's a bit of a mess,' she said.

'What?' he asked.

'The garden,' she replied.

'Methinks it were a happy life
    To be no better than a homely swain.'

'Absolutely,' she replied.

So Anne Hathaway lit a fire like she done in the old days. A fire that reminded her of the fire that burnt in Anne Hathaway's Cottage when they sat on the wooing seat so long ago and he wooed her and wed her and life seemed so simple.

And as Shakespeare slept and dreamt of snapdragons and walkways and colonnades and fennel, Anne Hathaway read his *Complete Works* to the very end and finally looked up with aged eyes just as the dawn touched the hem of her careworn Elizabethan farthingale.

'I am in great amazedness,' she said.

But so engrossed had she been that she had not noticed something extraordinary occurring. For while she read, William Shakespeare, Bard of all the Avons and Father of All Poesy, *was being borne slowly aloft*, carried up to the ceiling and gently transported out of the window by hundreds and hundreds of little miniature Shakespearean characters. A little tiny Julius Caesar at one foot and a little miniature Othello at the other, a miniscule Timon of Athens bearing his knees and, at his arms, a little Coriolanus, a miniature Henry IV Part 2, and a little Shylock with a tiny little Bottom and, at his elbows, a teeny little Elbow. And Lo! A Froth and a Romeo and Juliet and a Professor Higgins and a Lady Capulet and a Sir John O'Gielgud, and they all carried him higher and higher, further and further away until all they were was a dot like a skylark in the sky.

And suddenly a massive temple appeared in the clouds, full of pinnacles and towers and temple-haunting martlets and looking very similar to St Pancras Station, and Anne looked up, just in time to see his bald head disappear between two massive studded doors that slammed shut with a sound like thunder over a huge clump of elms next door to the Royal Shakespeare Theatre.

'*Absolutely typical!*' she said, listening once again to the familiar silence.

THINGS TO DO:

1. Explain the following: a) incremental repetition;
b) implicit metaphor; c) pyrrhic spondee; d) anapaestic tetrameter; e) sheltered accommodation; f) maternity benefit; g) Bramley's seedling; h) dinner lady;
i) Fortnum and Mason; j) sporran.

PART TWO

SHAKESPEARE: HOW TO DO IT

'Go bind up yon dangling apricocks'
(Shakespeare)

CHAPTER XXXII
SHAKESPEARE IN REHEARSAL:
CHOOSING YOUR SYSTEM

'The product of the union of the self with this numinous presence is wholeness.'

(Gerald Grotowski)

Introduction

One of the questions I am constantly being asked, particularly by youthful actors and actresses throughout the world is, 'What is your rehearsal system, or, to put it more technically, your "System of Rehearsal"?'

Choosing Your System

In order to answer this fascinating question let us first break it up into three essential parts:

a) What is the right 'System of Rehearsal' FOR YOU?
b) Is it dangerous NOT TO HAVE a 'System of Rehearsal'?

and MOST IMPORTANT OF ALL:

c) What actually IS a 'System of Rehearsal'?

7. *Shakespearean Games 1: Flogging a dead horse*
(See chapter XXXVI, 'Theatre Games')

So, first:

c) What actually IS a 'System of Rehearsal'?

A 'System of Rehearsal' is absolutely essential when rehearsing ANY play, particularly Shakespeare, and is basically *the mysterious communion that occurs between actor and director prior to the choosing of props and costumes.*

This mysterious communion is, in fact, so mysterious, not to say numinous, that very few actors or directors are prepared, or indeed able, to talk about it, *per se*. Harriet Walters, for instance, one of the most famous actresses in the world and one whose performances of endless Shakespearean heroines such as Rosmersholm and Bertram and so forth have made her very much a 'name to watch', stated, upon being asked to describe the mysterious and numinous communion that occurs between actor and audience, 'I'd rather not talk about it, *per se*.' Which clearly puts the whole problem very much in a nutshell, in my opinion.

And brings us on to our second question:

b) 'Is it dangerous NOT TO HAVE a "System of Rehearsal"?'

And the answer to this question, of course, is quite clearly YES, IN FACT *VERY* DANGEROUS. Because, if one is experiencing deep communion – on whatever level – certainly before choosing props and costumes, it is perilous, not to say irresponsible, to just do it willy-nilly.

Which brings us, of course, to the final question, or rather the *first* question, which is, 'What is the right "System of Rehearsal" *for you*?'

What is the right 'System of Rehearsal' for you?

And in answer to this aspect of this fascinating question I have decided to proffer a number of examples:

A number of examples

    1. *Polish Theatre*
    a) All actors sit in circle.
    b) Read-through.
    c) Tea or coffee and biscuits.
    d) Hopping games.
    e) End of rehearsal.

2. *Method*
a) All actors sit in circle.
b) Read-through.
c) Tea or coffee and biscuits.
d) Props given out.
e) Discuss Birth Traumas.
f) Warm-up games.
g) Company meeting.
h) End of rehearsal.

3. *Noh Theatre*
a) All actors sit in circle.
b) Read-through.
c) Saké and biscuits.
d) Try on Noh Masks. Or no masks (if not required).
e) End of rehearsal.

4. *Rough Theatre*
a) All actors sit in circle.
b) Go about room hitting other cast members.
c) Tea or coffee (no biscuits).
d) Form an intimate personal wholeness.
e) Lunch.
f) Find a partner.
g) Become frenzied.
h) Tea.
i) Read-through holding umbrellas.

WARNING!!!

ON NO ACCOUNT ATTEMPT ANY OF THE ABOVE 'SYSTEMS OF REHEARSAL' WITHOUT PROPER EXPERT SUPERVISION. *N.B. CHOOSING A REHEARSAL SYSTEM WITH UNDUE CARE AND ATTENTION CAN LEAD TO PROFESSIONAL RUIN AND EMOTIONAL BREAKDOWN.*

Conclusion

And so let us leave the essential world of 'Systems of Rehearsal' as we continue on our journey in the footsteps of the man who wrote 'What is Sylvia that all her swains commend her?' and 'Who are they that they shall beat out my brains with billets.' The Swan of Avon, in other words, or rather the 'Dirty Duck', as he was known to his friends.

THINGS TO DO:

1. Make Noh Masks for the following well-known Noh Plays: *Miss Saigon*; *Noh Noh Nanette*; *Noh Sex Please We're British*; *Noh Way to Treat a Lady*; *Seven Samurai*; *Seven Miles to Reno*.

2. Do this well-known Polish warm-up game:
   a) Turn into a bird;
   b) Take off in flight;
   c) Land.

CHAPTER XXXIII
SHAKESPEARE IN REHEARSAL:
LEARNING TO ACT

'Easier said than done.'

(Stanislavski)

Introduction
One of the most essential aspects of rehearsing Shakespeare, of course, is to learn how to act. In fact, until you have learnt how to do this fascinating skill, doing Shakespeare will remain a cruelly elusive dream, a tantalising spectre, always just out of reach. In fact, *I myself*, believe it or not, remember the days when my own personal ability to act was cruelly eluding me, not to say very much in doubt. In fact the idea of consummating any of the great Shakespearean roles such as Hamlet and Henry IV, Part 1 seemed then but a pitiless phantasm. 'When? O when?' I remember myself sobbing, 'will I be able to consummate Hamlet and Henry IV Part 1?'

A Moving Experience
As is well known, of course, I have now been fortunate enough to have consummated all of the great Shakespearean roles. And a deeply challenging and moving experience it has been too! At least

when I say 'all', I don't mean I've consummated *all* his roles as yet obviously. In other words, speaking as someone who came rather late (and somewhat reluctantly, if I may say so!) into the 'acting arena', I have always felt it was of the utmost importance to 'pace myself' so to speak, i.e. *not consummate everything in sight.*

Leading Exponent

Thus, while having mastered the art of Shakespearean acting, and acting generally obviously, and also being widely regarded as one of its leading exponents, I feel it has been the right decision not to actually do any whole plays in the public sector *at this stage.*

And this *for one crucial reason*, which I discovered recently whilst consummating certain Shakespearean sequences very much within the confines of my own room.

Enormous success

Needless to say, these sequences were consummated with enormous success and I, for one, was profoundly moved by the response. But, as I say, I did discover the following essential reason against doing the whole play or 'going the whole hog', as it is known, *too soon.* And it is a reason every incipient actor, studying for a major Shakespearean role, should be made aware of *before it is too late.*

YOU HAVE TO LEARN IT.

In other words, what you might not realise, and the modern audience generally has no idea of, is that every line being uttered on the contemporary stage has actually been LEARNED by the artist concerned.

So, needless to say, it came as a bit of a shock when I made the attempt, as part of my researches into the current volume, to actually 'learn the lines' of one of the most legendary of all Shakespearean roles, Henry V.

So what was the problem?

Let me say right away, of course, that the actual learning part wasn't the problem. In fact, I took to 'line-learning' as a duck takes to water. But what I found somewhat trickier and more complex was *retaining the learnt line in the mind.* Via 'brainal retention' as it is known.

Brainal Retention

In other words, I discovered that, having spent fifteen minutes becoming word perfect on the monarch's first line, i.e. 'O for a muse of fire that would ascend', when I tried to learn the second line, i.e. the line directly following the first line, i.e. 'the brightest heaven of invention', the first line quite suddenly and inexplicably *vanished*. Thus leaving me with a perfectly learnt second line, but no line preceding it, i.e. no 'O for a muse of fire that would ascend' to make sense of and give meaning to the second line, i.e. 'the brightest heaven of invention', i.e. *the line just learned*.

Great Truths

I had inadvertently stumbled upon one of the great truths of Shakespearean acting. Namely, that a *Shakespearean speech simply will not work unless one puts all the lines together*.

So what did I do?

I am not ashamed to admit that, to start with, I found myself somewhat despairing and even at certain moments lost my temper slightly and hurled the volume onto the floor and stamped on it which highly sensitive people with artistic temperaments have a tendency, not to say need, to do in certain key moments of 'creative stress'. Which is what this very much was, in my opinion.[1]

Then it was I remembered *an extremely crucial medical fact*.

Namely, that it has, in fact, been proved that if one is in more or less one's late thirties or early forties (which I happen to be in, believe it or not!) and one suddenly and without warning embarks on large stretches of line-learning when one has never done any form of line-learning before, i.e. in one's early years, then the shock to one's system is so massive that it is not only impossible to learn more than one line at the same time but also – and more important – actually *medically inadvisable*, not to say dangerous, for the brain to actually attempt it. *Which is why I stopped immediately*.

For the brain, and not many people realise this, has the retention capacity or 'retention centre' for *just so much and no more*. Particularly, if one is a deeply artistic person, who is also highly sensitive and has a

---

[1] Particularly when I discovered that the lines I had been attempting to memorise were not Henry V's at all but someone called Prol. In other words a complete and utter waste of time!

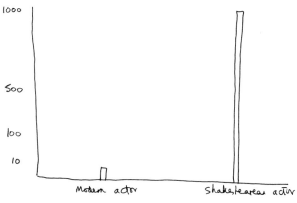

*Graph outlining 'brainal retention' abilities of the
Shakespearean actor as opposed to the modern actor*

lot of other problems *on his plate as well*, i.e. he *may well want to* learn a
Shakespeare play but, quite simply, can't.

Hardly Bears Thinking About

In other words, if the human orgasm was *meant* to retain a massive
amount more, then we would quite simply have been given massively bigger brains – the implication of which – i.e. massively
bigger heads – hardly bears thinking about.

Conclusion

So, in conclusion, it is crucial to realise this before attempting to
commit anything to memory and certainly anything as medically
dangerous as *an entire Shakespeare play*.

THINGS TO DO:

1. Make a papier mâché model of ONE of the following
human brains: i) An ordinary humdrum brain; ii) an
artistic and gifted brain; iii) an artistic and gifted brain
worrying about various problems of a personal and
financial nature.
2. Cry havoc.

CHAPTER XXXIV

SHAKESPEARE IN REHEARSAL:
CHARACTERISATION AND HOW TO DO IT

'So much has been said and written about characterisation!'

(Eric Morris – *Acting from the Ultimate Unconsciousness*)

ONE of the most essential aspects of 'learning to act' is to learn how to do 'characterisation'.

So how does one do 'characterisation'? And more to the point, what is it?

'Characterisation' and how to do it

'Characterisation' is basically the character you are playing, i.e. Henry VII, or Katherine Mansfield, which is all well and good obviously, but doesn't alter the far more complex question: How do we do it?

So how do we do it?

Basically, via two alternate but complementary methods which are as follows:

a) Reading the play.

b) Probing one's deep primal subconscious mechanisms, for which reading the play is useful *but by no means essential.*[1]

So one can do 'characterisation' without necessarily reading the play?

Yes you certainly can. In fact, very few people realise this and spend endless valuable hours toiling through various Shakespeare plays when they didn't need to.

So let us begin by looking at these two methods in more detail:

a) Reading the play.

If one decides to opt for the 'reading the play' approach, then what one does is look for various clues as to what form of characterisation one's character takes.

So where does one find these clues?

Well, the main clues, of course, are found in *The Stage Directions.*

So what are the stage directions when they're at home?

These are the extremely helpful long descriptive passages, before the play begins, which are extremely helpful in helping us know exactly where we are and who everybody is, and so forth and will read something like this:

ACT ONE

The attractive living room of 'The Oaks', the Georgian country home of SIR DAVID *and* LADY BARBARA MOUNTVIEW *on the evening of* HETTY MOUNTVIEW*'s twenty-first birthday. The large four-seater sofa and fabulous selection of antique furniture with which the room is furnished, and the Palladian French Windows that look across magnificent lawns towards the Thames glinting in the distance, tell us that the owners of the house are not short of a bob or two. Over the fireplace is a picture of Sir David's father,* SIR GEOFFREY MOUNTVIEW*, a cruel-looking man in a Safari suit holding a Zulu assegai, telling us that there may well be a tragedy before the end of Act Three. A matador outfit and three tennis*

---

[1] *My* italics.

8. *Four Shakespearean tragic heroes:*
Macbeth; Henry V; Julius Caesar; George III

rackets, however, lying on the fabulous four-seater sofa tell us that revelry is in the air and that the whole Mountview family and their young friends TONY CARTWRIGHT *and* ELAINE OSBORNE *and also the enigmatic but fabulously wealthy* LORD ROTHERMERE *are determined to make Hetty's twenty-first a night to remember. A fire roars in the fireplace and table lights glow amidst the leather-bound bookshelves. Only one thing, apart from the glowering portrait of Sir Geoffrey, gives us any cause for unease, in this idyllic scene. The inert and horribly contorted body of* LADY BARBARA. *An open clutch bag lying at her side.*

Suddenly we hear voices and laughter. The door stage left that leads to the huge baronial palladian entrance hall opens onto the sweeping regency driveway with its distant view of the English village of Fenminster. In runs HETTY MOUNTVIEW. *She is a young and frankly attractive girl wearing a fashionable primrose summer frock. She has sparkling blue eyes, a petite nose and full mouth that men find irresistible. Not to mention a mass of pre-Raphaelite curls and a perfectly formed full figure that belies her youthful years. Hetty is the only child of Sir David and Lady Barbara and has a somewhat headstrong nature that can become petulant when crossed. Otherwise she is a sweet and lovable girl who has just returned from studying art in Paris where she lived with the Dupont family, all of whom have recently died in a mysterious boating accident off the Cap d'Antibes. Hetty was cleared of all suspicion but memories of the tragedy, not to mention the months of relentless questioning by Interpol, have left their mark in an inescapable sadness around her eyes. Or is it sadness? Is it something darker? Is that the reason she never talks about Cap d'Antibes or indeed the Dupont family? And what happened to seventy-year-old Madame Dupont, whose body was never recovered? Could it be, in other words, that she has inherited the personality of her grandfather Sir Geoffrey with its tendency to obsessive lying and psychotic violence? And why is the gold inlaid Louis Quinze tallboy which stands facing the four-seater sofa and opposite the six original Chippendale dining chairs kept permanently locked? And why does she sob hysterically whenever anyone mentions her horse Hey Ho?*

HETTY walks in and pours herself a vodka and lemon from the Mountviews' well-stocked Regency drinks cabinet.

HETTY *(pouring herself a drink).* You are a clot, Tony! You know I absolutely loathe losing at anything! Particularly badminton. If you really love me and want to be engaged to me before the end of my twenty-first birthday, then you won't do that again in a hurry!

The living-room door opens and in walks TONY CARTWRIGHT. *He is handsome, debonair and an Oxford rowing blue, but with the hint of something not quite right about him.*

TONY (*walking in and pouring himself a drink*). Hey ho!

HETTY *begins to sob hysterically.*

TONY. Hetty darling!

HETTY. I thought you were referring to my horse.

TONY. Of course not. Not Hey Ho your horse.

HETTY *sobs.*

TONY. Just hey ho!

HETTY *runs from the room.*

TONY. So much for my matrimonial chances this evening!

Now, if one is playing Hetty, for instance, and wants to know how to do her characterisation, one needs to look no further than this, i.e. it's all there *on the page*, so to speak.

Unfortunately, however, Shakespeare does not use this form of stage direction. In fact, Shakespeare does not use any form of stage direction whatsoever. He simply has characters walk on without any kind of explanation or back-up information whatsoever, and the play *just starts!*

Needless to say this is one of the great mysteries of Shakespearean study and one that Shakespearean experts have battled over for centuries, i.e. why, for instance, when Henry V appears for the first time, does it say nothing more than:

Enter the KING, *accompanied by* GLOUCESTER, BEDFORD, CLARENCE, WARWICK, WESTMORELAND *and* EXTER.

and say ABSOLUTELY NOTHING, in other words, about the king or his personality or even what he looks like? What we might have hoped for would be something like:

Enter KING HENRY V *– a rugged warrior with a well-formed agile body without a hint of flab, a finely chiselled face and penetrating grey eyes that can terrify one moment and inspire the next. With the youthful* *impetuosity for which he is famed, he hurls open the palace doors and marches towards his splendidly carved throne on its gold dais beneath its spectacular clustre of ruched union jacks before swinging round and fixing the court with his steely gaze. Immediately, it is clear something is on the monarch's mind and it doesn't take an expert to know exactly what it is — namely the Conquest of France — and soon!*

THE KING *(impetuously drawing his sword).* Where is my Gracious Lord of Canterbury?

ARCHBISHOP OF CANTERBURY. Here my liege!

THE KING *(hurling his crown across the floor impetuously).* We must invade France!

ARCHBISHOP OF CANTERBURY. We invaded France last year, my liege.

THE KING *(fixing the* ARCHBISHOP *with his steely grin).* So what!

ARCHBISHOP OF CANTERBURY *(realising he'd better give in to this charismatic, chisel-jawed monarch whose grave wisdom belies his youthful years).* Absolutely, your Highness.

The Court cheers. Exeunt.

So why is it that Shakespeare never wrote this form of stage directions thus assisting the actors in the difficult task of doing characterisation?

Unfortunately, we shall never know, which brings us to our second means of doing characterisation, namely:

b) Probing one's deep primal subconscious mechanisms

Which is unfortunately all we have time for at the moment.

Conclusion
And so let us now move on to the fascinating world of blocking.

THINGS TO DO:

1. Explore THREE of the following: a) Henry V; b) Katherine Mansfield; c) Mansfield Park; d) Mansfield Road; e) Mansfield Notts.
2. Let slip the dogs of war.

CHAPTER XXXV
HOW WE DO THE BLOCKING

'Do not block me, old mole!'

(Shakespeare)

ONE of the questions I am regularly asked as an artistic director is 'How do we do the "blocking"?' Or, to put it another way: 'What is "blocking", basically?'

In other words, and to be perfectly blunt, if you are an artistic director and *don't know what 'blocking' is*, you are likely to have a very rough ride indeed.

You may, for instance, overhear the following perfectly innocent conversation between two incipient actors:

'What did you do in rehearsal today then?'

'We worked out how our "blocking" went.'

'So how is the "blocking" then, in your opinion?'

'It is very good "blocking" in my opinion and will help us all immeasurably in the weeks to come.'

and have *absolutely no idea* what on earth they're talking about.

So is it easy to find out?

Yes, I'm happy to say that after a bit of rooting around in various shops and so forth, it is certainly possible to find out what 'blocking' is, more or less.

So what actually is it, then?

The 'blocking', believe it or not, is in fact knowing where all the characters go, basically.

I beg your pardon?

Where all the characters go, basically.

When?

Sorry?

Go when?

When they're 'on stage', so to speak.

I see. So why do all the characters need to know where to go when they're 'on stage', so to speak?

Unfortunately, the answer to this particular query I have not been able to discover at this juncture, but suffice it to say if they don't, the whole play is liable to *fall to pieces*.

Which one should avoid at all costs, presumably?

Exactly!

So how come the actors can't work out what the 'blocking' is for themselves?

I must admit I was also somewhat surprised that actors can't work it out for themselves, but apparently they can't, and that's where we come in.

Who?

Artistic directors.

So how do we do the 'blocking' then?

By using the 'Blocking Charts'.

Charts on which to put the 'blocking'?

Precisely. Large charts on which to put the 'blocking'.

I see.

You then show the charts to the actors who then do what's on the charts, basically.

And say no more about it?

If you're lucky.

Do you ever show the charts to the audience?

Only if the two actors have a mid-performance 'blocking disagreement' and you need a third opinion.

Finally, do you have any examples?

Examples of 'Blocking Charts', as they're known?

Yes, if possible.

I do, as it happens. Here, in fact, are a number of 'Blocking Charts' for *Hamlet* and *Othello*, which will be useful, not only to the incipient actor but also to the burgeoning artistic director hopefully.

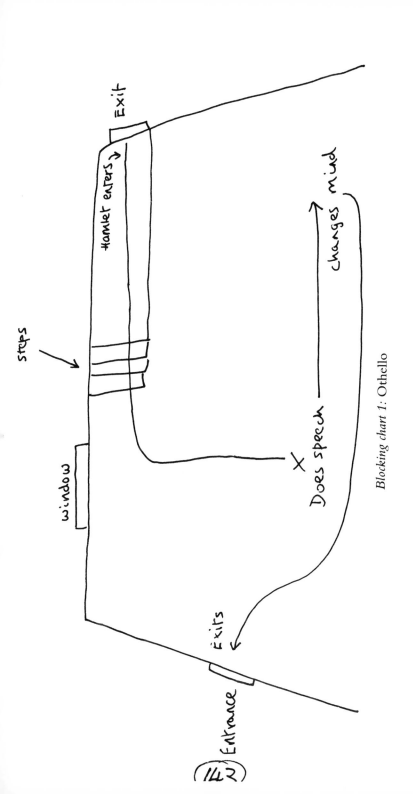

Blocking chart 1: Othello

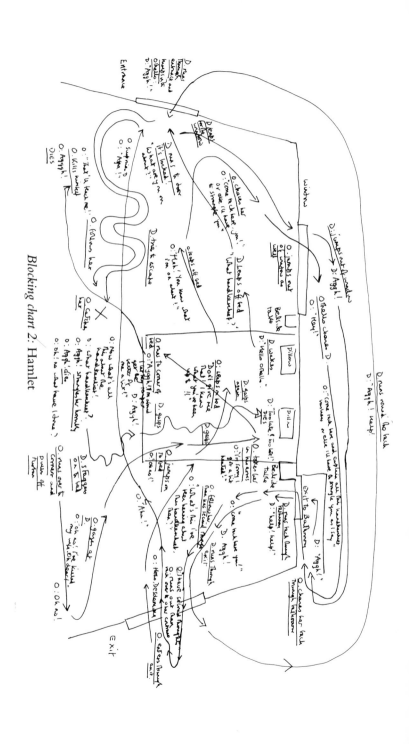

Blocking chart 2: Hamlet

CHAPTER XXXVI
THEATRE GAMES FOR SHAKESPEAREAN ACTING

'He knows the game. How true he keeps the wind.'

(Shakespeare)

Introduction

I – along with many other well-known artistic directors – hold an enormous amount of truck with *Theatre Games* which are an invaluable aid to a number of things, such as releasing the Inner Unconscious and clearing Unpleasant Blockages.

Why Theatre Games?

So let us now look at *Theatre Games* in detail and examine, not only their basic function, but also their essential purpose within the overall structure of the Rehearsal Process.

What are Theatre Games?

Theatre Games are either played in a circle (Circle Games), in a line (Line Games), on a table (Table Games) or in the dark (Adult Games). Also there are other games like Hunt the Kipper.

Some further Theatre Games

Finally, here are some further *Theatre Games* which are also handy:

a) Wham the Sligo
b) Musical Spoons
c) Up Jenkins!
d) Duck the Orange
e) Flog the dead horse.

Fig. 1   *Fig. 2*

Two well-known warm-up games

Conclusion

And so it can be seen that, by a constant use of *Theatre Games*, your Blockages and numerous other things can be considerably improved and aided.

THINGS TO DO:

1. Breed a Tudor rose.

2. Weld an Elizabethan pewter tankard.

3. Flog a dead horse.

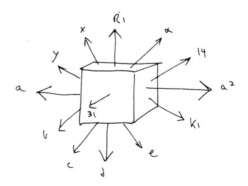

Diagram of actor's space orientation: the Kinesthetic Cube (or Sphere)

CHAPTER XXXVII
SHAKESPEARE AND THE BODY:
THE CORRECT USE OF THE BODY IN SHAKESPEARE

'Open your vowels at least twice a day.'

(Stanislavski)

NEEDLESS to say it is impossible to successfully enact Shake-speare until one has achieved correct bodily alignment. In the accompanying visual aid, the author demonstrates how to achieve 'correct bodily alignment' (see over).

N.B. It is important not to rush 'correct bodily alignment'. I only achieved mine after months of intensive training. But it can be done! In fact, 'bodily alignment' experts inform me that I am a leading example of this fascinating condition.

THINGS TO DO:

1. Sew an Elizabethan farthingale.

9. Correct bodily alignment

CHAPTER XXXVIII
THE VERSE PROBLEM –
AND HOW TO MASTER IT

'Many a mickle makes a muckle.'

(Jonson & Johnson)

Introduction

Which brings us to one of the most critical problems for the Shakespearean actor. Namely, the verse problem.

So how do we master the verse problem and more to the point what is the verse problem?

The Verse Problem

Unfortunately nobody is quite sure what the Verse Problem is exactly, which makes 'Mastering the Verse Problem' a slightly trickier 'nut to crack' than it would be if we did obviously. Suffice it to say, however, that it causes havoc in numerous regional and West End theatres and can usually be spotted by a number of 'tell-tale symptoms' such as contrapuntal off-beats, dissonant rhyming mechanisms, alliterative assonants and, worst of all, irregular vowel movements, which can cause serious, not to say agonising, problems for the emergent actor.[1]

---

[1] Not surprisingly.

Here anyway are some 'Useful Exercises when Attempting Verse' which I have personally found extremely helpful.

Some Useful Exercises when Attempting Verse

1. Keep calm.
2. Lie on the floor and take three deep breaths followed by 149 short breaths without pause for three hours.
3. Shake out ankles, rib cage and lower intestine and above all – *relax*! And finally:
4. Good luck!

THINGS TO DO:

1. Write an essay describing what you would do with THREE of the following: a) ouphes; b) statute caps; c) woosel; d) vantbrace.

2. Caper nimbly in a lady's chamber.

10. Mastering the verse

CHAPTER XXXIX

THE RIGHT AND WRONG WAY TO PLAY A ROLE

or

APPROACHING JULIUS CAESAR

'Who is't?'
''Tis me.'
'Who art thou?'
'Julius Caesar.'
'Approach Julius Caesar!'
'Thank you.'

(*Julius Caesar*,
Act V, sc ii.)

ONE of the things that artistic directors such as myself, Sir Peter Hall, Sir Richard Eyres and so forth get asked pretty much most of the time is what are the right and wrong ways to play a role.

In fact, artistic directors generally agree that this is very much one of the hazards of the job, i.e. actors coming up at various inopportune moments, in the corridor, during an important promotional business lunch or what have you, to ask whether they should play a particular role *this* way or *that* way or in fact how on earth they should play it, in our opinion. Now let me say at the outset that we don't mind, obviously, seeing as we all see this as very much 'part of the job', but to pester us day in, day out, with no self-restraint whatsoever, can only lead to bitterness, resentment and, in particular, *diminished feedback*.

In fact, when actors complain of this well-known complaint the reason is nearly always due to the above reason, i.e. what is termed by artistic directors, such as Sir Peter Hall, Sir Trevor Nunn, Sir Richard Eyres and so forth as *over-pushy role querying*.

Anyway, having said that, what do we say to the actor who says to us:

'What are the right and wrong ways to play this role?'

And what we say to him is that he is in fact asking *the wrong question*. The question he *should* be asking is: 'What are the right and wrong ways to *approach this part?*'

And *instantly* – the reader will notice – the problem virtually vanishes.

So now we've cleared that up, thank goodness, how, in fact, should we 'approach our parts'?

For the purposes of this illustration, let us suppose, for a moment, that the parts we are talking about are not any old parts or 'random parts' as they are known technically, but parts in the well-known play *Julius Caesar*. And, in particular, the most well-known part of *Julius Caesar* which of course is Julius Caesar.

Now supposing you've been offered this part and you want to know 'how to approach it'.

Well, firstly, you say to yourself, 'I have been offered the part of Julius Caesar. How should I approach it?'

Then, very slowly, *approach* it.

It's as simple as that!

But with one *very important warning*:

JULIUS CAESAR DIES HALFWAY THROUGH.

Yes! The whole of the rest of the play (THREE WHOLE ACTS believe it or not!) is everybody else – *but not him!*

Why Shakespeare decided to kill off his central character at this point in the play we can only guess, but as I say, I feel it is only fair to warn the 'approaching' actor before it is too late. Yes – it is disappointing and I'm truly sorry. But better you discover it now than discover it *when there is no turning back*. At the read-through, for example or – even worse – ON THE FIRST NIGHT!

Fortunately, however, there is a solution. Namely, a new

version of *Julius Caesar* written by myself, as it happens, and based on the original version by William Shakespeare but with the following 'change of plot'. Namely that Julius Caesar *doesn't die*.

We pick it up at Act III, scene i, line 74:

CAES. Hence! Wilt thou lift up Olympus?

DEC. Great Caesar –

CAES. Doth not Brutus bootless kneel?

CASCA. Speak hands for me!

> *The conspirators all attempt to stab* CAESAR, *but* CAESAR *swings round and deftly parries the attack.*

CAES. What? Wouldst murder the Emperor? *(He parries.)* Ha! Have at you! *(And thrusts.)* Ha!

CASCA *(dies)*. Ah!

CAES. Ha! *(He thrusts again.)*

DEC *(dies)*. Aggh!

CAES. Aha!

CASS *(dies)*. Aggggh!

CAES. That'll teach you! *(He thrusts.)*

MET *(dies)*. AGGGGGGH!

CAES. Ho! Ho! *(He parries and thrusts, shins up a column and swings down on a rope.* BRUTUS *cowers.)*

BRUT. Forgive me, my emperor!

CAES. Not the *last* emperor, I'm happy to say! *(He holds his sword aloft.)* Aha!

BRUT. Not me too, your Highness!

CAES. Yes! You too, Brute! *(*CAESAR *stabs* BRUTUS.*)*

BRUT *(dies)*. Agggggh!

CAES. Liberty! Freedom! Tyranny is dead!

> *Enter* GUARD.

154

GUARD. Hooray!

CAES. Where are the Roman populace, guard?

GUARD. Weeping and sobbing, your Royal Highness!

CAES. Then go proclaim this to the sobbing mob!

GUARD. What?

CAES. To chuck their sweaty nightcaps in the air!

GUARD. Hooray!

Exit GUARD. *Enter* MOB, *chucking sweaty nightcaps in the air.*

MOB. Hooray!

CAES. Guard?

Enter GUARD.

GUARD. Yes, your Highness?

CAES. Here they are.

GUARD. Who, your Highness?

CAES. The sweaty mob.

GUARD. Hooray!

Exit GUARD.

CAES. Now list my speech.

MOB. We will, your Highness.

CAES. But first –

MOB. Yes, your Highness?

CAES. Would you mind not throwing your sweaty nightcaps in the air?

MOB. Certainly.

The MOB *stop chucking their sweaty nightcaps in the air.*

CAES. Thank you.

The MOB *waits.*

MOB. Speak the speech, I pray you, trippingly on the tongue!

CAES. Friends, Romans, Countrymen, lend me your ears.

Pause.

MOB. Marvellous!

CAES. Thank you very much.

MOB. What a speech!

REST OF MOB. Fabulous!

Exeunt omnes.

CURTAIN

Thus ends my 'new version' of *Julius Caesar*. Not only missing out the last three inessential acts, but also giving the play a much-needed 'shot in the arm' in my opinion and making it ideally suited for performance by schools, OAPs, pre-school play groups, etc.

Finally, I hope I have demonstrated how – with only a small degree of imagination – it is possible to turn even one of the Bard's most glaring errors into an astonishingly relevant 'play for today' and an invaluable part of the modern world repertoire. Particularly abroad.[1]

Production of Julius Caesar

THINGS TO DO:

1. Describe in your own words ONE of the following: 'Diminished feedback'; 'Brutus'; 'Sir Richard Eyres'.

2. Caper nimbly in a lady's chamber.

---

[1] Such as in Australia and New Zealand where audiences are renowned for not following any play for longer than three and a half minutes.

CHAPTER XL

HOW TO ACT SHAKESPEARE: AN INTERVIEW WITH A WELL-KNOWN PRIMA DONNA
JULIET STEVENSON INTERVIEWED BY DESMOND OLIVIER DINGLE

'Old and young, we are all on our last cruise.'

(Robert Louis Stevenson)

MISS Juliet Stevenson and I met 'over coffee' in a discreet Soho restaurant. She arrived on the dot of twelve, looking slightly fragile, slightly disconcerted, in fact every inch the well-known Prima Donna which she certainly is, of course.

DESMOND OLIVIER DINGLE. Firstly, I should like to thank Miss Juliet Stevenson most profusely for taking time out of her extremely busy schedule in the very busy world she inhabits doing numerous films and so forth, not to mention –

JULIET STEVENSON. Thank you.

DESMOND OLIVIER DINGLE. Thank you. Anyway, the first question I think the reader would be interested in knowing is when you are 'approaching a Shakespearean role', so to speak –

JULIET STEVENSON. Yes?

DESMOND OLIVIER DINGLE. How do you learn the lines?

JULIET STEVENSON. The lines?

DESMOND OLIVIER DINGLE. How do you learn them?

Pause.

JULIET STEVENSON. Well, it just comes naturally, I suppose. It's just –

DESMOND OLIVIER DINGLE. I mean do you use an envelope, or the back of a book or what?

JULIET STEVENSON. Can we change the subject?

DESMOND OLIVIER DINGLE. Absolutely.

JULIET STEVENSON. Thank you.

DESMOND OLIVIER DINGLE. How do you join the Royal Shakespeare Company?

JULIET STEVENSON. What?

DESMOND OLIVIER DINGLE. Or the RSC obviously?

JULIET STEVENSON. How do you join?

DESMOND OLIVIER DINGLE. Generally.

JULIET STEVENSON. You're asked.

DESMOND OLIVIER DINGLE. Asked?

JULIET STEVENSON *(laughs)*. Of course!!

DESMOND OLIVIER DINGLE *(laughs)*. Absolutely!!

JULIET STEVENSON. Now, can we talk about something else, please?

DESMOND OLIVIER DINGLE. Certainly. (*Pause.*) And the next question which I'm sure will intrigue your many fans throughout the world is how do you do the 'Curtain Calls'?

JULIET STEVENSON. Curtain calls?

DESMOND OLIVIER DINGLE. Is it a kind of . . . telepathy?

JULIET STEVENSON. *What?*

DESMOND OLIVIER DINGLE. How you all bow at the same time?

Pause.

JULIET STEVENSON. You start from the centre and move out.

DESMOND OLIVIER DINGLE. Sorry?

JULIET STEVENSON. It fans out from the centre!!

DESMOND OLIVIER DINGLE. Fans?

JULIET STEVENSON. Jesus! WHEN THE PERSON NEXT TO YOU BOWS THEN YOU BOW!

DESMOND OLIVIER DINGLE. Marvellous.

JULIET STEVENSON. JESUS! *(Pause.)* What about my acting?

DESMOND OLIVIER DINGLE. Your what?

JULIET STEVENSON. ACTING!!

DESMOND OLIVIER DINGLE. Acting. Absolutely. How do you do the blood?

JULIET STEVENSON. Blood?

DESMOND OLIVIER DINGLE. In battles?

JULIET STEVENSON. Blood in battles?

DESMOND OLIVIER DINGLE. Do you hide it? In a kind of pouch? Or is it more –

JULIET STEVENSON. I HAVE NO IDEA HOW THEY DO THE BLOOD IN BATTLES!!! I'VE NEVER BEEN IN A BLOODY BATTLE!!

Pause.

DESMOND OLIVIER DINGLE. Fabulous.

WAITER. Madame?

JULIET STEVENSON. NEVER EVER EVER BEEN IN A BLOODY BLOODY BLOODY BATTLE!!!

DESMOND OLIVIER DINGLE. And finally –

JULIET STEVENSON. NEVER NEVER NEVER NEVER NEVER NEVER!!

DESMOND OLIVIER DINGLE. – Are you by any chance any relation to Robert Louis Stevenson?

JULIET STEVENSON. Call me a cab.

DESMOND OLIVIER DINGLE. Or –

JULIET STEVENSON. Cab.

WAITER. Madame?

DESMOND OLIVIER DINGLE. Right.

JULIET STEVENSON. CAB!

DESMOND OLIVIER DINGLE. Thank you.

JULIET STEVENSON. CAB! CAB! CAB! CAB! CAB! CAB! CAB! CAB! CAB! CAB!

MANAGER. Madame?

DESMOND OLIVIER DINGLE. Absolutely.

The interview ended after what truly was a fascinating insight into the legendary world of one of our most famous actresses.

Australian production of Julius Caesar

CHAPTER XLI
DOING THE PROPS

'Miss Heather Conway is certainly a reliable guide. During the nine years we worked together at the British Drama League, I came to know how skilful she was with her hands.'

(E. Martin Browne CBE)

Introduction

One of the most essential aspects of Shakespeare is the props. In fact it is now universally agreed by artistic directors across the globe that Shakespeare wrote nearly all of his plays actually *around the props*. In other words, it was the props that inspired the piece (and not vice versa as is generally supposed).

Quick Glance

Take a quick glance at any of his major works and you'll see exactly what I mean. *Gammer Gurton's Needle*, *Arsenic and Old Lace*, and *A Doll's House* are all stiff with props as their titles imply and immeasurably enhanced as a result. Not every play, of course. Some plays have virtually no props whatsoever, such as *Much Ado About Nothing* and *No Orchids for Miss Blandish* but – as a general rule with Shakespeare – the play is the props. Or – as he himself put it in *Troilism and Cressida* – 'the props is the play'.

So what are we saying exactly?

161

SHAKESPEARE: THE TRUTH

We're saying it is essential to get the props right.

Off Course

In fact, if you *don't* get the props right, the likelihood is you'll find whole scenes, not to mention entire plays, sailing hopelessly off course and totally foundering before the audience is barely out of the foyer. In fact, when experts and underwriters examine the wreckage of a production which *has* sailed hopelessly off course and totally foundered, the root cause is *virtually always* lack of proper prop provision or 'inadequate propping' as it is known, technically.

Let us examine this theorem, therefore, in the light of a number of leading Shakespearean plays. And imagine them – for our purposes – *without the props.*

Meaningless Nonsense

'Is this a dagger which I see before me?' asks Hamlet, for instance, in one of the most famous scenes in theatrical parlance.

It is indeed. But imagine this famous sequence WITHOUT THE DAGGER!

Would it not be unthinkable?

I BELIEVE IT WOULD.

Or:

'A horse, a horse, my Kingdom for a horse!!'

as Richard Crouch End weeps – understandably – for his horse, the legendary Black Beauty.

But what if there were *NO HORSE*!! What if Black Beauty FAILED TO LEAP from the burning stables at Birtwick Park at the end of Act V?

We'd have a very different play indeed. And a disappointing one at that, in my opinion!

Car Park

But let Sir Peter Brook have the last word: 'Make no mistake – *Richard II* without Black Beauty and the audience would be back in that car park WITHIN SECONDS!'

To which I would add (if I may): '*And who's to blame them?*'

In other words, to put no finer point to it, without the props the play is dead.

162

So how actually do we 'do the props' if we are an artistic director?

The answer is almost absurd in its childlike simplicity. We simply *make a list*.

Here, for instance, is Sir Richard Eyres:

'Before I direct any Shakespeare play, I simply make a list.'

Or Sir Peter Brook, again:

'Always always always get that props list under your belt first. After that, it's downhill *all the way*!'

Which brings us to the next crucial question:

So should one hire props or make them?

This debate has, of course, raged throughout the theatre for centuries. Nowadays, however, almost all of our leading artistic directors agree that home-made props is best. Here is Sir Trevor Nunn, for example:

'I certainly stand by the home-made prop!'

Or his charming wife, Imogen (or 'George' as she is affectionately known) Stubbs.

'I fell in love with Sir Trev, not only because he sired my child which I don't mind admitting, but also because he makes all his own props which is remarkable when you consider everything else he has to do when mounting a play. The baby was a bonus, obviously, but it was Trev's props that finally clinched it and turned us into a "going concern"!'

So – as a general rule – when considering Shakespearean props the rule is a simple one:

MAKE YOUR OWN.

So are there any useful tips when making Shakespearean props?

Yes, there certainly are. In fact make sure that you READ THESE TIPS THOROUGHLY BEFORE ATTEMPTING ANY PROP CONSTRUCTION.

a) Become proficient with hessian, copper tubing, galvanised clay, raffia, marble chips and – of course – perforated zinc.

163

b) Take care with mock weapons. In particular the guisarme and large-scale siege engines.

c) Never use gloss paint on mock fruit. This can slip if inexpertly handled, resulting in unpleasant mid-play mishaps, such as hitting or, worse still, being eaten by members of the audience. The latter leading – often tragically – to MOCK FRUIT POISONING (*see tip d) below*).

d) Never eat mock fruit while you are *on stage*. This leads to a considerably worse version of the above (*see above*), i.e. *ON-STAGE* MOCK FRUIT POISONING which – actors and managers agree – is without doubt the most unpleasant on-stage fatality one can possibly hope to get. In other words, of all forms of theatrical death, poisoning certainly takes the biscuit! Not only because the victim generally takes up to twenty minutes of horrendous convulsions before finally pegging out, but also because it LOOKS so unpleasant in the centre of a brightly lit stage. Particularly during a matinee. In fact, many's the time a theatre manager has had an entire audience of OAPs trooping out *mid-performance* to demand their money back because an actor has died on stage – often mid-speech – from a particularly ghastly attack of fatal toxic mock-food poisoning. So what should be done if such an incident occurred? One way, of course, would be for the other actors to try and solve this fairly common problem by 'improvising round it', as it is termed. But even the most gifted extemporisers would be hard put to it to ad-lib their way round some situations. Here, for example, is a common one:

Enter LADY CAPULET.

LA. CAP. Nurse, where's my daughter Juliet? Call her forth to me.

NURSE. Certainly, your Highness, I bade her come. What, Juliet! Where's this girl? Juliet, I say?

Enter JULIET.

JUL. How now? Who calls?

JULIET *taketh apple and nonchalantly taketh a massive bite.*

NURSE. Your mother.

JUL. Madam, I am here, what is your will?

LA. CAP. This is the matter.

JULIET *maketh to answer, then convulses and drops dead.*

[In this situation, the actors might attempt to continue with the last four and a half acts *without* Juliet, but this would stretch credulity somewhat, particularly with her horribly contorted body lying there throughout. Probably it would be best to cut straight to Lady Capulet's last line in Act Five, borrow a couple more from *Hamlet* and end the play thus:]

LA. CAP. Oh me! this sight of death is as a bell
That warms my old age to a sepulchre.

NURSE. But here comes Romeo, Lady Capulet.

LA. CAP. Oh no, not one of our well-known enemies!

NURSE. He's not as bad as all that, your Highness.

LA. CAP. I suppose not. In fact I've probably been a bit intolerant recently. Along with my husband Lord Capulet.

NURSE. No no no!

LA. CAP. Haven't I?

NURSE. Well perhaps a bit.

Enter ROMEO.

LA. CAP. Hello, Romeo.

ROMEO. Hello, Lady Capulet.

Fig. iii. Mock fruit

LA. CAP. I'm afraid Juliet's dead. As you can see.

ROMEO. Yes I certainly can see. I loved her, Horatio.
   She was likely, had she been put on,
   To have proved most royal.

LA. CAP. She certainly would.

NURSE. Anyway, go bid the soldiers shoot!

ROMEO. All right then.

   Exeunt (marching; after which a peal of ordnance are shot off).[1]

So, as you embark on combing through the text and making your first props list, are there any other tips it would be handy to know about before embarking?

   Yes. Probably the most important tip of all. Which is, of course:

KNOW YOUR EPOCH

That is to say, it is essential to know whether your production should be:

   EITHER a) Shakespearean
   OR b) Modern Dress.

Once you have decided on this critical decision, you're nearly *home and dry*!

   Here, for instance, are two props lists drawn up by myself for *Macbeth*, or 'The Scottish Play' as it is known.

PROPS LISTS FOR WELL-KNOWN 'SCOTTISH PLAY'

SHAKESPEAREAN	MODERN DRESS
One cauldron.	Cigarette lighter.
One dagger (suspended).	One dart board.
Three swords.	One bottle Glenfiddick.
Ninety earthenware bowls.	One Epson lap-top computer.
One moving wood.	One pint semi-skimmed milk.
One rook.	One set garden furniture.

---

[1] N.B. Avoid eating 'peal of ordnance', needless to say.

DOING THE PROPS

One porter.
One drum.
Fifteen beards.
One temple-haunting martlet.
One brief candle.
One maggot-pie.
One chough.
One caber.
One cream-faced loon.
One newt's eye.
One lizard's leg.
Bat wool.
Turk's nose.
Finger of birth-strangled babe.
Seventeen sporrans.
One haggis.

One packet Kleenex.
One angle-poise lamp.
One false nose.

THINGS TO DO:

1. Make the following props in less than fifteen seconds:
Samian earthenware pot; papier mâché zinc-padded
Celtic goblet; Assyrian chariot; winged Persian griffin;
Byzantine church; mediaeval glaive; cuirass; and an
Egyptian toilet.

2. Answer at least THREE of the following essay
questions: 1. Why would you use a 'maund'? 2. Where
would you put a 'pilum'? 3. What would you do then?

3. Write short notes on NO MORE THAN FOUR of
the following phrases: i) 'Paddock calls'; ii) 'Anon'.

a) *What you need*

b) *Are you ready?*

c) *Make your papier mâché 1*

d) *Make your papier mâché 2*

e) *Make your papier mâché 3*

f) *Make your helmet*

g) *The final touches*

h) *Bob's your uncle!*

11. How to make a simple Shakespearean helmet

PART THREE

SHAKESPEARE: YOUR PROBLEMS SOLVED

'Женщины не прощают неуспеха.'

(Chekhov)

CHAPTER XLII
SHAKESPEAREAN COMEDY –
AND HOW TO SPOT IT

'He is a man of comedy virtues,
Nor did he soil the fact with cowardice.'

(*Timon of Athens*, Act III; scene v; line 141)

SHAKESPEARE, as we know, wrote numerous well-known comedies which are, of course, some of the most amusing plays ever written. In fact, one mention of the word 'Shakespearean Comedy' and audiences find themselves rolling in the aisles almost immediately. I know I certainly do.

But for those readers who are *still* unconvinced, in other words, those amongst you who can sit through an uproarious piece of Shakespearean quippage such as *As You Like It* and not be basically helpless by the end, here are a number of major examples which should certainly prove my point.

'Come shepherd, let us make an honourable retreat, though not with bag and baggage, yet with scrip and scribbage.'

Or this one, which always makes me laugh:

'I'll graff it with you, and then I shall graff it with a medlar. Then it will be the earliest fruit i' the country; for you'll be rotten ere be

171

half ripe, and that's the right virtue of the medlar.'

Another marvellous line. Or:

'That codding spirit had they from their mother,
As sure a card as ever won the set.'[1]

Which is unfortunately all we have time for at the moment.

And so, finally, how do we tell when a Shakespearean play is a 'Shakespearean Comedy' and when it isn't?

In other words, how do we *spot the comedy*?

To do this, simply look out for the following tell-tale signs:

1) An Amusing *title*, such as *As You Like It*, for instance. 'A title that has you chuckling means a play that'll have you chortling' is a helpful rule of thumb in my experience and one used by many experts.

b) Numerous *quips*. Quips are humorous Shakespearean sayings which are generally extremely amusing whilst also being totally incomprehensible (i.e. 'I was never so berhymed since Pythagoras' time, that I was an Irish rat, which I can hardly remember'). Fortunately, however, quips generally mean only one thing. Unlike puns which mean several (see below). Which brings us to:

c) *Puns* (or 'Shakespearean Puns', as they are known). Puns, of course, are the same as quips but with many more meanings, as we have already heard (*see above*). Each new meaning proving an even more amusing meaning than the last meaning, if you get my meaning. Here, for example, is a well-known example of a 'Shakespearean Pun': 'The trouble with monks is they never get out of their dirty *habits*' (*The Winslow Boy* V; iv; 769) which is not only positively brimming with meanings but is also extremely amusing.

d) Other amusing Shakespearean *words*, including 'caper', 'scant', 'pish', 'cuckoldy ram', 'baubling vessel' and 'bare bodkin'.

---

[1] Unfortunately, it has recently come to my attention that this humorous quip in fact comes from the well-known play *Titus Andronicus* which is one of the most gratuitously violent and unpleasant of all Shakespeare's works and therefore not exactly a comedy, as such. However, I am sure the reader – having read the above – will agree that it was an easy mistake for the author to have made and is probably wondering even now why on earth it doesn't in fact come from a 'Shakespearean Comedy'. Tragically, we shall probably never know.

Naturally, there are other more complex methods of 'comedy spotting' that we don't have time to explore at this juncture and, anyway, would be of little interest to the layman, but, generally speaking – with the above guidelines at one's beck and call, so to speak, when entering the Mighty Arena of 'Shakespearean Comedy' – *one can't go far wrong.*

Cuckoldy ram

THINGS TO DO:

1. Read the following Shakespeare plays and spot which ones are 'Shakespearean Comedies' (if any): *A Little of What You Fancy*; *Henry VI, Part 3*; *Robinson Crusoe*.

2. Write an essay on AT LEAST ONE of the following subjects:
    a) 'Shakespearean Comedy in a nutshell';
    b) 'Shakespearean Comedy, as I see it';
    c) 'Shakespearean Comedy – or is it?'

3. Write a Shakespearean quip including ALL the following words: 'hodge-pudding', 'smulkin', 'blag', 'arch-mock', 'wooden pricks', 'trundle-tail' and 'internal organ'.

CHAPTER XLIII
HAMLET RECONSIDERED

'Alas poor Yorick'

(Ralph Roister-Doister)

IT is generally essential to reconsider Hamlet at all times. And I – along with many other well known literary experts – certainly do so whenever possible.

Unfortunately, owing to various unforeseen contingencies, I still haven't had an opportunity to do this as yet but very much hope to do so in the very near future.

THINGS TO DO:

1. Make an Elizabethan ruff.

SHAKESPEARE FOR MODERN AUDIENCES: 1
The Tragedy of *Othello*
by
WILLIAM SHAKESPEARE
A modern verse rendition
by
DESMOND OLIVIER DINGLE

ACT ONE

Scene: A street in Vienna. Enter OTHELLO *and* DESDEMONA.

DESDEMONA. Welcome, noble Moor!

OTHELLO. Ah! My lovely wife Desdemona!

DESDEMONA. Good trip?

OTHELLO. Yes, thank you very much.

Enter IAGO.

IAGO. Hello from me too, by the way.

OTHELLO. Hello Iago. This is my wife Desdemona, by the way.

IAGO. Hello Desdemona.

DESDEMONA. Hello, Iago.

IAGO. Anyway, don't mind me.

OTHELLO. Sorry?

IAGO. I just need to check a couple of things.

OTHELLO. Fair enough.

   IAGO *checks a number of maps, pens and papers etc. in the bureau.*

OTHELLO. Anyway, I hope you have been true to me!

DESDEMONA. I beg your pardon?

OTHELLO. While I've been away in various wars in Cyprus?

DESDEMONA. Of course I have, my noble Moor.

OTHELLO. Because if you haven't, I may be driven mad!

DESDEMONA. Good heavens! I didn't realise that about your personality!

IAGO *(aside)*. Nor did I!

OTHELLO. *And* strangle you on your bed!

DESDEMONA. Good Lord!

OTHELLO. So no hanky-panky!

DESDEMONA. Pardon?

OTHELLO. With a handkerchief, for instance!

DESDEMONA. Hanky-panky with a handkerchief?

OTHELLO. Hanky-panky with a hanky!

DESDEMONA. Keep your hair on!

IAGO *(aside)*. Good heavens!

   An awkward moment.

OTHELLO. I'm sorry!

DESDEMONA. Blimey!

OTHELLO. I'm a little overwrought.

DESDEMONA. I'll say!

Another awkward moment. IAGO *continues checking the bureau.*

IAGO. Anyway . . .

OTHELLO. I humbly do beseech you of your pardon
For too much loving you.

DESDEMONA. Right.

Another awkward moment. They look at one another.

OTHELLO. So have you got it?

DESDEMONA. What?

OTHELLO. The hanky!

DESDEMONA. The hanky?

OTHELLO. You haven't got it?

DESDEMONA. *NO!!*

OTHELLO. So who has got it?

DESDEMONA. I DON'T KNOW WHO'S GOT IT!!

OTHELLO. Right, that's it!

DESDEMONA. What?

OTHELLO *strangles* DESDEMONA.

DESDEMONA. Agggh!

IAGO *is still checking the bureau.*

IAGO. Don't mind me.

OTHELLO. What have I done?

INTERVAL

ACT FIVE

A few seconds later. Enter BRABANTIO, THE DOGE OF VENICE *and* GIORGIO ARMANI.

GIORGIO ARMANI. What has happened?

OTHELLO. It is the very error of the moon.
  She comes more near the earth than she was wont
  And makes men mad.

ALL. A likely story!

  They murder OTHELLO.

OTHELLO. Agggggh!

  Exeunt BRABANTIO, THE DOGE OF VENICE *and* GIORGIO ARMANI.
  There is an awkward silence.

IAGO. So . . . er . . .

  Re-enter BRABANTIO, THE DOGE OF VENICE *and* GIORGIO ARMANI.

GIORGIO ARMANI. What?

IAGO. . . . thanks to all at once and to each one,
  Whom we invite to see us crowned at Scone.

  A slight pause.

ALL. Marvellous.

  Exeunt BRABANTIO, THE DOGE OF VENICE *and* GIORGIO ARMANI.
  Exeunt IAGO, *having closed the bureau.*

FINIS

The Doge of Venice

CHAPTER XLIV
THE ELIZABETHAN BODY
An Approach to Elizabethan Medicine and the Elizabethan Body

'Pocohontas' body, lovely as a poplar, sweet as a red haw in November or a pawpaw in May.'

(Cool Tombs)

WARNING

Unfortunately, due to the graphic nature of the subject of this chapter, readers with nervous, medical or emotional difficulties should move on immediately to page 182.

Let us pause, at this juncture, to examine in detail the Elizabethan body. And ask ourselves a number of essential medical questions that need to be addressed whilst examining Shakespeare's corpus.

1. What was the Elizabethan body and what did it contain?

Apart from the brain and various bones and so forth, the Elizabethan – or Tudor – body contained very little else apart from four extremely unpleasant fluids or 'humours'. Needless to say, these fluids or humours were so unpleasant, not to say disgusting, that they are now, in fact, believed to be one of the central reasons behind the Tudors' early demise.

2. So what exactly were the 'Tudor fluids or humours' and – more important – were they in fact that funny?

Unfortunately, we shall never know, but suffice it to say that they were generally secreted somewhere between the large intestine, the gall bladder and the St Pancras area, and had an unpleasant habit of flooding the human orgasm at the slightest provocation, quite often in public, and causing havoc throughout the Elizabethan World Picture.

3. So was there any form of medicine that the Elizabethans did to combat complications arising from the four well-known humorous Tudor fluids (see above)?

Yes, there were four basic methods of Elizabethan medicine, namely 'cupping', 'crouping', 'emetic infusions' and the application of a fowl after the plucking out of its tail feathers.

4. What exactly happened when a fowl was applied without its tail feathers?

I'd rather not say, at this juncture.

5. And finally, were there many other forms of Elizabethan diseases during the Tudor Epoch?

Yes, there were a number of other popular forms of Elizabethan diseases, many of which are too unpleasant to mention, but the chief ones were as follows, basically:

a) painful malady
b) grievous cholic
c) erratick fever
d) morbid trunk
e) face ache
f) turning into a wolf
g) the Plague.

Which brings us to the last essential aspect of Elizabethan medicine, namely the Plague.

6. The Plague

The biggest problem for Elizabethan health workers was, of course, the Plague which was so infectious that an entire audience of 20,000 people watching the first performance of *Love's Labours Lost* in 1598 contracted the disease from an irresponsible programme seller as they went in and were stone dead by the interval.

A Tudor turning into a wolf

Somewhat disconcerting for the actors, naturally, many of whom had not performed in public before, being straight out of drama school, and thus found it a slightly unnerving, not to say demoralising, first night, to walk out for the second half into what was, quite literally, a 'dead house'. First nights are never easy at the best of times, of course, but this one must have truly 'taken the biscuit'.

THINGS TO DO:

1. Practise self-emetic infusion.

2. Turn into a wolf.

SHAKESPEARE FOR MODERN AUDIENCES: 2
The famed 'To Be or Not To Be' scene from
Hamlet
by
WILLIAM SHAKESPEARE
A modern verse rendition
by
DESMOND OLIVIER DINGLE

ACT ONE

Scene: A street in Denmark. Enter HAMLET.

HAMLET. To be or not to be.
   That is the problem as I see it at this juncture, basically.
   Whether it is nobler in the mind to suffer
   All the set-backs and what-not that occur, generally speaking,
   Through life.
   Put up with the whole bleeding treadmill, in other words, or
      simply
   Jack it in.
   To die, to sleep – no more,
   That's what's on my mind, basically.
   I could say if I done this, obviously,

182

12. Othello

I'd have no more concerns, no more personal problems or
Financial constraints.
But,
On the other hand,
I'd be dead.
Which is a bit of a problem
When you think about it.

Exeunt.

CHAPTER XLV
SHAKESPEARE ON RADIO

'Mrs Carter could make a pudding as well as translate Epictetus.'

(Jonson & Johnson)

A sensitive issue
We now come to the sensitive issue of Shakespeare on radio. And I'm afraid the less said about this topic the better in my opinion. In other words, although many have tried to make Shakespeare work on radio, it doesn't.

Serious error
This is mainly due to the fact that Shakespeare is famed first and foremost as a visual medium. And so to have *just his words* without any form of props or 'scenic back-up' whatsoever is in my opinion a *very serious error indeed*. As I'm sure the Bard would have been the first to agree.

Audience hatred
In short, audiences throughout the world hate Shakespeare on the radio. And – to be honest – who's to blame them?

Conclusion
I'm sorry I have been compelled to close this chapter on a controversial note but, if Shakespeare had wanted his plays on the radio, surely he would have *written radio plays*!

SHAKESPEARE: THE TRUTH

THINGS TO DO:

1. Write a radio play entitled EITHER: 'Mrs Burningham's Day Out' OR: 'How Are We Going to Tell Dotty?'

2. Write an essay entitled: 'Where would we be without radio?'

CHAPTER XLVI
SHAKESPEARE ON TELEVISION

'For saucefleem he was withe eyen narwe.'

(Sir William Caxton)

Introduction
Shakespeare, of course, works consideraby better on television.

Conclusion
Which is a bit of luck for people who can't get out much. And you can also *turn over*, obviously, which is an added bonus.

THINGS TO DO:

1. Rewrite this chapter as an eleven-line Rondelet.

2. Design a mural entitled: 'What would we do without television?'

CHAPTER XLVII

SHAKESPEARE ON FILM

'Oh Chatterton, how very sad thy fate!
Dear child of sorrow! Son of misery!
How soon the film of death obscured that eye
Whence genius wildly flashed.'

(Keats)

Introduction
Shakespeare – although very much a live medium obviously –
certainly lends himself to the magical art of film. In fact, numerous
well-known Shakespeare films have been made and for this reason
are known as Shakespeare on Film.

Some well-known Shakespeare films
These include *Henry V*, *Spartacus*, *The Lion in Winter* and *Howard's
End*. Besides numerous other films as well such as *The Eagle Has
Landed* and *Marnie*.

So what are the advantages of doing Shakespeare on Film?

Advantages
Clearly there are many superb advantages of doing Shakespeare on
Film, which are as follows:

a) You can do indentical twin scenes, i.e. have both twins talking *at the same time*, via using the well-known 'split screen' technique.[1]

b) You can do *realistic blood, and beheadings*. (N.B. For a crucial and fascinating analysis of how they do the blood in Shakespeare, turn back to Chapter XLI, 'An Interview with a Well-Known Prima Donna'.)

c) Films are less boring.

Lawrence of Arabia

Disadvantages of Shakespeare on Film

Unfortunately, however, there are also numerous disadvantages of doing Shakespeare on Film as well, which are so numerous as to be virtually impossible to list in a volume of this size.[2]

In other words, although Shakespeare certainly does work on film, he also often doesn't, in my opinion. And I would strongly urge the reader to take this into consideration when considering doing Shakespeare on Film.

In other words, if the reader is considering doing Shakespeare on Film, suffice it for me to proffer ONE word of warning:

DON'T!

THINGS *NOT* TO DO:

1. Make a film of a Shakespeare play.

---

[1] Also triplets, quadruplets and even quintets, obviously, such as *The Raj Quartet*, Schubert's *Octet in F Major* and *Quintet for One*.

[2] Which is also Lord Methuen's opinion, as it happens, as I have just been personally informed by his Lordship in a fascinating 'internal memorandum' on the subject of the present chapter, which has in fact led me to an invaluable 'further analysis' of a number of opinions raised in the chapter, seeing as it is in fact my firm opinion that it is more important to see 'both sides of every coin', as it were, than just see one simply because it happens to be someone's opinion. Hence I am delighted to place on record Lord Methuen's opinion, with which I happen to almost entirely concur, as it happens, having had a chance to think about it a bit.

CHAPTER XLVIII

SHAKESPEARE AND THE BIRTH OF THE ENGLISH LANGUAGE

'The language that came from nowhere and now is spoken by millions.'

(Robert McCrumb)

The English Language – A Short History

What is the English Language? And how did it begin? And more to the point how did it become – almost overnight – what it is today? *Namely, the most major and sought-after language the world has ever known.*

1. It is now recognised by nearly every leading linguistic expert in the world that, of all global languages, English is the language that foreign people freely confess is the language they wish they'd been born with *instead of their own mother tongue.*[1]

2. It is now in fact believed that a number of Germans and

---

[1] And is of course another reason why Canadian, New Zealand and Australian people for instance are so grateful to be part of the British Commonwealth, i.e. because they are able – despite the fact that they are so far away – to speak English *every day of their lives* without so much as batting an eyelid.

13. *Shakespearean Fights
and Combats 2:
The quarterstaff*

Danish, for instance, have actually 'come out' and admitted that they wished they didn't speak German or Danish at all, but English. And not simply because nobody understands what on earth they're on about whenever they ask the way somewhere but chiefly because their own languages, i.e. German and Danish, actually *sound extremely unpleasant.*

E.T.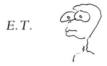

3. Many German and Danish poets for instance, such as Goethe, Ibsen and Timberlake Wertenbaker, actually rue the day they was born German and Danish simply because they don't have the colossal linguistic advantages we have. In other words, the realisation that, due to a simple *quirk of birth*, the greatest language in the world has been denied them must be a source of almost unendurable pain. And explains:

> a) Why foreign works can't hold a candle to English ones, basically.
> b) Why the U.K. has more famous writers *per capita* in ratio to its acreage than any other country in the world.
> c) Why the Germano–Danish races are famed generally only for their music, such as Beethoven and yodelling.

So how did this extraordinary language, i.e. English, come about?

It came about, of course, through one man. His name: William Shakespeare.

A well-known fact

It is a well-known fact, of course, that William Shakespeare, besides inventing many crucial linguistic devices such as the octosyllabic couplet and fellatio, also invented some of the most beauteous passages in the English language.

Shakespeare's Passages

Unfortunately, we do not have time to examine Shakespeare's passages in detail at this juncture. Suffice it to say, however, that without his passages the world would have been a very different place indeed.

On the map

What is less well known, however, although it's hardly surprising when you think about it, is that Shakespeare also invented the *English language*. More or less putting it on the map, so to speak, *virtually single-handed*.

So how did this in fact come about?

And the answer, of course, is that it came about through the Coming of the Mighty Tudors.

The coming of the mighty Tudors

In fact, if it hadn't been for the coming of the mighty Tudors in 1308, the English language might well have sunk without trace and English men and women would be walking about even today without having any idea what anybody else was on about.[1]

An ordinary man

For it was with the advent of the coming of the mighty Tudors, of course, that a man was born in Stratford-upon-Avon. An ordinary man. A simple man. A simple ordinary Tudor man. A man you might pass in the street and give not a second glance to. Nothing unusual, in other words. Nothing, apart from his peculiarly large domed head, particularly odd or abnormal.

Or was there?

Wasn't there *something else* about this apparently perfectly ordinary yet, at the same time, strangely enigmatic Midlands glove salesman?

And if so – what?

Finger on it

For a while, try as they may, no one could quite put their finger on it. Even his wife couldn't put her finger on it, despite the fact that they'd been married for four years. In fact, night after night in those little wattle-and-daub huts clustered on the banks of the mighty rushing Avon, everybody was trying to put their finger on it. But all without success.

---

[1] I have recently been informed, as a matter of interest, that the Tudors of England were in fact Welsh. This came as a bit of a shock – as it will to many readers – and is still under investigation by myself. But, whatever the case, when they became Tudor they very generously put all that behind them and became English. As they are to this day, obviously. Apart from Lord Snowdon, Lord Caernarvon and the Prince of Wales, of course, who is also Duchess of Cornwall.

They knew there was something. But what was it?

What was it that set him apart?

And then – one day – the truth dawned.

THAT MAN FROM STRATFORD-UPON-AVON
SPOKE A COMPLETELY DIFFERENT LANGUAGE.

A language – they swiftly realised – that was for all mankind!!

The Railway Children

Wigan wigheardne

How refreshing it must have been when suddenly, after centuries of:

Scyldburh tobrecon. Abreode his angin
Wigan wigheardne, se waes haten Wulfstan,
On wklancan pam wicge, paet waere hit ure hlaford

people suddenly heard:

If music be the food of love, play on!

echoing down their Tudor cobbles. Or:

Civet is of a baser birth than tar,
the very uncleanly flux of a cat.

They may not have understood what he was on about but at least they could spell it.

And that was the important thing!

Conclusion

In fact, it is astonishing that so many words that we now take so much for granted, such as 'tights', 'hose', 'thigh-boots', 'russet', 'mantle', 'clad' and 'cladding' in fact all came from his extraordinary and teeming mind.

In other words, not for nothing is he called 'Father of All Mankind'.

THINGS TO DO:

1. Make a papier mâché model of ONE of the following: Lord Snowdon; Timberlake Wertenbaker; Wigan Wigheardne.

2. Do a diorama entitled EITHER: 'The Coming of the Mighty Tudors' OR: 'Shakespeare's Wife Puts Her Finger On It'.

SHAKESPEARE FOR MODERN AUDIENCES: 3
Richard II
by
WILLIAM SHAKESPEARE
A modern verse rendition
by
DESMOND OLIVIER DINGLE

ACT ONE

Scene: Buckingham Palace. Enter RICHARD II.

RICHARD II. I am Richard II, as you know.

   Enter BUSHY.

BUSHY. You certainly are and no mistake.

   Enter HENRY IV.

RICHARD II. But who is this when he's at home?

HENRY IV. Henry.

RICHARD II. Henry what?

HENRY IV. Henry the Fourth!

RICHARD II. Henry the Fourth *what?*

HENRY IV. Henry the Fourth, Part One.

The court gasp.

RICHARD II. Then banished wilt thou be these fourscore years.

HENRY IV. Fourscore years!

BUSHY. That will teach you!

HENRY IV. I'll be back.

RICHARD II. Pish!

BUSHY. Well said, your Highness!

Exeunt HENRY IV, PART 1. *Enter* JOHN OF GAUNT.

JOHN OF GAUNT. This silver jewel set in a silver sea!

RICHARD II. Absolutely.

Exeunt JOHN OF GAUNT. *Enter* BUSHY *with* BAGOT.

BAGOT. I'm afraid Bushy's got some bad news.

Enter HENRY IV, PART 2.

HENRY IV. Here I am back again!

The court gasp.

HENRY IV. Henry the Fourth, Part Two!

RICHARD II. Oh no!

ACT TWO

Scene: Balmoral. A few days later.

HENRY IV. As I was saying –

RICHARD II *(to* BAGOT*).* Sorry who are you again?

BAGOT. Bagot.

RICHARD II. So who's Bushy?

BUSHY. I'm Bushy.

HENRY IV. I have returned!

RICHARD II. So who's Scroop?

GREEN. Scroop?

HENRY IV. Henry the Fourth, Part Two!

The court gasp.

ACT THREE

Scene: Flint Castle. A few years later.

RICHARD II. Berkley Castle call they this at hand?

Enter HENRY IV, PART 2.

HENRY IV. YES! AND THAT'S JUST WHERE YOU'RE GOING!

RICHARD II. Oh no!

BAGOT. Chin up, your Majesty.

RICHARD II. You won't leave me?

BUSHY. Never, your Highness.

RICHARD II. Thank you.

RICHARD enters castle. Dies.

BUSHY. Good riddance!

BAGOT. Ha! Ha!

GREEN. Absolutely!

HATCH END. That's what I always thought!

HENRY IV, PART 2. Hooray!

ALL. Hooray Henry!

Flourish. Tuckets without. Exeunt omnes.

FINIS

CHAPTER XLIX

THE BIRTH OF THE CRITICS

"πῶς," ἔφη, "ὦ Σοφόκλεις, ἔχεις πρὸς τἀφροδίσια; ἔτι οἷός τε εἶ γυναικὶ συγγίγνεσθαι;" καὶ ὅς, "εὐφήμει," ἔφη, "ὦ ἄνθρωπε. ἀσμενέστατα μέντοι αὐτὸ ἀπέφυγον, ωσπερ λυττῶντά τινα καὶ ἄγριον δεσπότην ἀποδράς."

[It's all Greek to me.]
(Herodotus)

A S I sit here at my desk in my director's suite, I find that I am at this moment actually glancing at *The Times* of Friday March 5th 1993. I have, in fact, just bought it, as a matter of interest, from my local 'corner shop'. And, whilst looking at it, a number of things have in fact struck me, pertaining to this volume.

But first, allow me to answer a number of 'reader's queries' that I imagine you will probably be having at this moment.

Why did I buy The Times?

The Times is of course probably the most prestigious newspaper in the known world and one taken by such people as the Queen, the Queen Mother, Prince Charles, the Archbishop of Canterbury etc. Not to mention foreign dignitaries such as the President of France and the Pope and so forth, all of whom READ *THE TIMES* FIRST not only because they are probably *in* it, but seeing as they reckon it gives them the most impartial view of what is going on in the world. Hence I buy *The Times*, for obvious reasons.

So when did The Times *start then?*

The Times started back in the fourteenth century, virtually the same time as Shakespeare did, fascinatingly enough.

So is that just coincidence?

No it isn't, as it happens. Intriguingly – and not many people realise this – The Times Newspapers Ltd actually began as a result of Shakespeare.

So did Shakespeare start The Times Newspapers, *then?*

In a sense, yes.

How come?

Well, despite the fact that Shakespeare's plays were getting more and more numerous at the Royal Shakespeare Theatre, the Tudor recession – as a result of the Spanish Armada and the Plague and so forth – was biting *so deep* that the emergent Tudor audience wanted to know what plays to spend its money on. But how were they to know?

Hence the creation of The Critics.

So how did the Critics begin then?

We shall never know exactly, of course, but I believe they may well have begun as a result of a typical Stratford-upon-Avon breakfast conversation, such as this.

'Shall we go to the RSC tonight?'
'Certainly, mine wife, what wouldst see?'
'*Othello* looks very good. Judging from the poster.'
'Posters aren't everything.'
'You're right there, mine housband.'
'How about *Measure For Measure*?'
'Is that a comedy or tragedy?'
'I think it's more one of his Problem Plays.'
'What, like *Timon of Athens*?'
'Yes.'

'Mmmm. I was none too keen on that.'

'Mmmm. Nor me neither.'

'If only there was some kind of special person who was employed to go to all the plays and say what *they* thought.'

'Who we could read you mean?'

'Aye.'

'That's a very good idea, mine housbounde.'

'Thank you. But what could we call him?'

'We could call him "the critic"?'

'That way we'd run a lesser risk of going to see rubbish.'

'Exactly. But where would we read the "critic"?'

'That's a good point. How about in a kind of "paper"?'

'A "paper"?'

'A large folding sheet.'

'That's a good idea. But would there be sufficient interest to make this scheme economically viable?'

'I have an idea!'

'What?'

'We could make it a special paper with all sorts of various items of new or recent interest.'

'But what could we call it?'

'We could call it a "new paper".'

'Or how about a "*news* paper"?'

'If there was more than one recent item of interest you mean?'

'Exactly!'

'Good idea! But where would the critic go then?'

'On a kind of Arts Page.'

'In the middle?'

'Well slightly after the middle.'

'Between Home Finance and Sport?'

'Exactly.'

'What a good idea, mine housenboundene.'

'Thank you very much.'

So finally did any other 'newspapers' start at this time or was it just The Times?

In fact, as a result of this idea, quite a number of leading newspapers started at this time. The *Daily Telegraph*, of course, the *Daily Express*, the *Mail on Sunday*, to name but a few. In fact, if we look at the headlines of today's papers, i.e. *The Times*, we notice how little has in fact changed in the world since the Elizabethan Epoch. How much, in fact, *Shakespeare himself would have recognised*:

QUEEN ILL
HISTORIC BUILDINGS EXPOSED TO UNNECESSARY FIRE RISKS
BEN JOHNSON BANNED FOR LIFE
WRONG FISH DESTROYED BY FRENCH
BALDNESS DROVE MAN TO ROBBERY
LABOUR LOSES IN LAMBETH

And so forth. Thus it can be seen that our worlds are in fact not so very distant.

Or are they?

This morning, I happened to notice a fascinating headline that would have been *unthinkable* in Shakespeare's Epoch.

It is, in fact, *the* headline of this morning's *Times* – with the astonishing wording:

MAJOR ASKS PUBLIC FOR HONOURS NOMINATIONS

Which is, of course, the revolutionary new system of proposing people for knighthoods etc., i.e. that it's basically no longer up to Her Majesty the Queen to spot people in the public eye and nominate them for knighthoods. Instead, it is now possible for *any* member of the public to nominate anybody who they personally think is worthy of 'the greatest honours of the realm', so to speak, such as the OBE, CBE, Knighthood, Order of the Bath, Marquis, Viscount and so forth. Not every Tom, Dick and Harry, obviously, but people who possibly might not have been suggested when it was the Queen who did it, but could just stand a chance now it's up to the public.

People, in other words, who have possibly had humble beginnings but who have worked and toiled their way into the public limelight, such as via a literary work such as this, for instance. Not in order to blow their own trumpets or gild their own larders, obviously, but as part of their service to the community, for the greater good of mankind and the Commonwealth.

What you should do

If you happen to know of an author or artistic director or someone who you believe is worthy of appearing on the Prime Minister's Honours List in the near future, then simply write down their name, occupation, why you feel they are particularly worthy and their publisher and send it STRAIGHT AWAY to:

> The Honours List Dept,
> The Prime Minister,
> 10 Downing Street,
> London W1.

Finally, what's in it for you?

Obviously, you would be doing this as a service to the community and so would seek no reward. However, it is possible that if your application *was* successful and the successful nominee was a well-known author, for example, then the author's publisher might be prevailed upon, in his retirement home or wherever he happened to be, to shell out, so to speak, a number of attractively signed 'free copies' of this volume (and *other volumes* possibly by other well-known writers, such as various Horror Stories etc.). Obviously, I can't promise anything at this stage, but I believe that having a knighted author on their books is something that could do Methuen's *quite a bit of good*, if you get my meaning.

Conclusion

And so it was the Tudor Epoch saw the Birth of the Critics almost entirely, not to say *entirely*, as a result of Shakespeare.

THINGS TO DO:

1. Do the above, as soon as possible (see above).

CHAPTER L

WAS SHAKESPEARE REALLY SHAKESPEARE?
An issue not to be shirked

'Now draw up Faustus like a foggy mist.'

(Philip Marlowe)

SHORTLY after I began my researches into William Shakespeare and the Tudor Epoch, an incident occurred one February afternoon that I am not ashamed to admit left me very profoundly shocked indeed. So shocked, in fact, that it very nearly shook the mighty foundations of the volume you currently hold in your hand. Indeed, it is conceivable that, as a result, I might have laid down my pen there and then and ceased my toiling forthwith.

Fortunately, I did not, however.

In fact I am happy to say that probably nothing could prevent the current œuvre from emerging – albeit with agonising slowness – from the bowel-like womb of my labours into the glorious sunlight of critical and popular acclaim.

But it could have.

In other words, what I'm saying is it very nearly did. But didn't, fortunately. Which is a bit of luck for all concerned, if I may say so. Not least Methuen's.

14. Shakespeare's hair-loss difficulty

A Profound Shock

So, anyway, what actually *did* happen that drear and melancholy lunchtime that caused such a profound, not to say seismic, shock while, at the same time, very nearly costing the reader the volume he – or she – is currently holding? Basically it was as follows.

I happened to be 'browsing' in the 'bargain basement' of a renowned London second-hand bookshop looking for various research materials on the current volume, when I happened to chance upon an ancient and leathern volume with barely audible faded gold lettering glinting on its spine. Impulsively, I reached up and withdrew it from where it had clearly lain undisturbed for centuries.

And then it was I saw its title.

Suddenly all extraneous sounds of the bustling metropolis teeming above me was hushed and immediately I wished I had 'left well alone' so to speak, not to say 'passed by on the other side'.

For the leathern-bound volume I was holding in my hand was entitled *Shakespeare was Bacon*.

Immediately, I thrust it back into the cobwebbed recess from whence I had withdrawn it and stood there a moment doing a number of complicated yoga exercises in order to regain my decomposed equilibrium.

A Worse Shock

Then – as if impelled by an unseen hand – I plucked forth another book from the same shelf.

For a moment, all seemed well and my equilibrium returned swiftly to its normal composium. For the volume I now had in my hand was entitled *A MAN CALLED SHAKESPEARE*.

'Thank goodness!' I heard myself exclaim as I opened this new volume at a place at random.

And then suddenly – *it happened again.*

Sorry Saga

Once again, all extraneous noise fell to a ghastly silence. This time even worse than before. In fact, it was without doubt the worst moment in the whole of this sorry saga, not to say volume. For *Shakespeare was Bacon* had NOTHING on what I now saw before me.

Staring up at me from those oh! so innocent seeming pages of what I now realise was *ironically* called *A MAN CALLED SHAKE-SPEARE* were the following words cruelly mocking me with their dreadful, not to say heart-stopping, simplicity:

'For let us be quite clear. The works of William Shakespeare are written by one man and one man only – Christopher Marlowe – the True Bard of Avon.'

Immediately, I knew there was only one thing to do. And I did it without compunction.

I complained to the Manager.

The Truth
So what is the Truth?

Or rather, what is the 'Truth behind the Bard'? Will we ever find out? Or does he still remain 'shrouded in mystery'?

Flyover
And the Truth is that just because I had a very unpleasant experience in a second-hand bookshop doesn't mean that *Shakespeare wasn't Shakespeare*. Everybody has unpleasant experiences in second-hand bookshops every day of the week, but that doesn't mean their whole life's purpose is rendered totally meaningless, does it? Anyway, Shakespeare couldn't have been Marlowe because Marlowe died under the Deptford Flyover. And Bacon couldn't have written him, seeing as if he'd been Bacon, we'd have had not the RSC but the RBC, in other words *The Royal Bacon Company*! And it's somewhat hard to imagine audiences the world over flocking to see the Royal Bacon Company, to be honest. Unless you're Danish, obviously.

Sundry
But the point is we all *know* why all and sundry went round saying they was William Shakespeare whenever they felt like it *and let's not beat about the bush here*.

Royalties
It was because of the Swan of Avon's massive royalties situation.[1] Which must have been colossal when you think about it. A staggering residuals situation that HARDLY BEARS THINKING ABOUT, in other words. With all the plays he wrote all day long and *no competition whatsoever* apart from *Gammer Gurton's Needle* and *Colin Clout Come Home Again*!, he must have had *so much cash coming in daily* he'd never have to work again! And they all knew that!!

---

[1] And the subject, of course, of the popular West End hit, *The Royalty Hunt of the Swan* by Sir Peter Parker (pub. Methuen Playtexts £1.95).

Cash Registers

Not that that's why *he* did it, obviously. The Bard himself wrote his *Works* not because of all the fabulous residuals and repeat fees he knew he was getting, but because he was deeply impelled by an irresistible fire winnowed by inner promptings from whence we know not. In other words, where a lesser writer might have penned the three parts of *Henry VI, Part 3* into the early hours with the sounds of cash registers ringing in his ears, William Shakespeare most certainly *did not*.

Despair

But let us not 'ring down the curtain' in a mood of despair. Let us instead finally finish this endless volume on a lighter note.

Lighter Note

For I can unequivocally state that I have personally examined much of Shakespeare and many of his *Works* also and I can now safely say that it is definitely my deep and abiding belief that the Truth behind William Shakespeare – Sun of Olde England, Immortal Swan, Bard of Avon, Tyne and Wear, Comedy of Errors and Mull of Kintyre – is as follows: Shakespeare was definitely Shakespeare in my opinion.

But let us let Him have the final word:

> They Truth then be they Dower.

Whatever that may mean.

THINGS TO DO:

1. Make the following simple Elizabethan junket:
    1. Take eight pints of milk.
    2. Add a pinch of hyssop.
    3. Finely chop four large French onions.
    4. Whisk milk until turned.
    5. Add four slices of ham.
    6. Take three pomanders.
    7. Fillet three halibuts.
    8. Grill vanilla pods over low flame.
    9. Souse for three hours.
    10. Serve with roast saddle of hare.

15. The author examining some Shakespearean text

SHAKESPEARE FOR MODERN AUDIENCES: 4

The famed 'Our Revels Now Have Ended' scene from *The Tempest*

by

WILLIAM SHAKESPEARE
A modern verse rendition
by
DESMOND OLIVIER DINGLE

ACT ONE

Scene: A Street in the Bermoothes.

Enter PROSPERO, FERDINAND *and* CARMEN MIRANDA.

PROSPERO. You do look, my son, in a movèd sort.

PRINCE FERDINAND. Do I?

PROSPERO. As if you were dismay'd.

PRINCE FERDINAND. Well I am a bit, to be honest.

PROSPERO. Be cheerful sir!

CARMEN MIRANDA. Loos'n up!

PRINCE FERDINAND *(bright'ning)*. Rightio.

PROSPERO. Our revels –

Invisible music is heard.

PRINCE FERDINAND *(amaz'd)*. What's that?

PROSPERO. Ariel.

FERDINAND II OF SPAIN *(more amaz'd)*. But it just . . . happened.

PROSPERO. It's automatic. Our revels –

ARCHDUKE FERDINAND OF AUSTRIA. Good Lord!

PROSPERO. Can I carry on?

EMPEROR FERDINAND OF THE BALKANS. Certainly.

PROSPERO. Our revels now are end'd and these our actors
   Or rather artistes (as I did actually say) –

FERDINAND III OF BOHEMIA AND NAPLES. What?

PROSPERO. (Say they would.)

FERDINAND IX OF BISSYNIA, BESSARABIA, MEXICO AND THE CANARY
   ISLANDS. Absolutely.

PROSPERO. Have all totally disappear'd more or less
   Into air,
   Or rather, to be more specific,
   Into thin air;
   And – like the baseless basic fabric
   Of this so-called basic vision basically –
   The great globe itself, yea the whole shebang,
   (i.e. various palaces and clouds and so forth)
   Shall completely and utterly vanish, so to speak
   And leave
   Not a rack behind. 'Cos
   We've had our good times
   We've had our bad times,
   But I love you just the way you are.
   And we've bin down all our highways,
   Our low days and our lay-bys,
   And I did it My Way,
   But there's always a tomorrow
   And tomorrow and tomorrow

Ariel

And our little life is rounded with a sleep.
Hey there!
Our little life is rounded with a sleep.
Thank you.

FERDINAND VII OF BRAZIL *(applauding)*. Fabulous!

PROSPERO. Thank you.

FERDINAND X OF BULGARIA, SAXE–COBURG AND BATTENBURG. First rate!

PROSPERO. You're not just saying that?

POPE FERDINAND XII. Good Heavens, no!

PROSPERO *(picking up the glistening apparel)*. Would you mind taking some of this?

FERDINAND DE LESSEPS BUILDER OF THE SUEZ CANAL. Not at all!

PROSPERO. Thank you very much.

CROWN PRINCE RUDOLPH. And where do we exeunt?

PROSPERO. Just here.

EDWARD THE CONFESSOR. Thank you.

Exeunt. Tuckets within.

FINIS

The Suez Canal

PART FOUR

A GLOSSARY OF SHAKESPEAREAN TERMS

'A shining gloss that vadeth suddenly.'
(Shakespeare)

GLOSSARY

Prithee	Outside Elizabethan lavatory.
Tights	See panty-hose.
Faggot	a) Delicious meaty dumpling.
	b) Form of rustic fire-lighter.
Codpiece	Rudimentary Elizabethan condom.
Frolic	Small lacy garment worn in private regions by gentlemen.
Essex	a) Home of well-known Earl.
	b) Attractive county North of London.
Ilford	Attractive and internationally renowned cultural centre of above.
Puke	Unpleasant activity carried out by infants.
Mewl	See puke. Particularly unpleasant when carried out simultaneously with above.
Tearoom	See Anne Hathaway.
Bodkin	Form of Elizabethan tea-cake. On sale at above.
Bare Bodkin	Same as above but unbuttered.
Elizabethan Tandoori	Popular restaurant on A23.
Bawd	Elizabethan construction material.
Bawdy House	House built of bawds.
Half-bawd	House half built of bawds.
Tobacco	Discovered by Sir Walter Raleigh.
Havana	Form of tobacco discovered by Sir Walter Raleigh.
Panatella	Form of Elizabethan trouser.
Slim Panatella	Form of above, for thin people.
Walter Raleigh	Famous caped Elizabethan smoker.
Raleigh	Reliable Elizabethan bicycle.
Hose	Elizabethan socks.
Panty-hose	Brief often black lacy Elizabethan underwear, combined with Elizabethan socks.

Pizzle	Sense of fun and exhilaration (e.g. 'on the pizzle').
Pizzled	Unrelated to above. Used by Australian characters (e.g. Lord Melbourne in *Henry IV, Part 3*) particularly when bewildered or confused about something, e.g. a plot point.
Tush	Painful sexual complaint.
Sour ringlets	Small rather bitter cocktail snacks.
Arthur's Bosom	Unfortunate complaint afflicting certain elderly actors.
Rialto	Popular name for cinema.
Trocadero	Popular name for shopping centre (see Leicester Square).
Arndale	See above.
Paddock calls	Anon.
Chattel	Succulent central part of pig's trotter.
Glibbery	a) Sensation of anxiety before a battle, conference or wooing. As in *Julius Caesar* V; iii: 'Where is my Lord of Shrewsbury?' 'He is feeling somewhat glibbery, my liege!' b) Collective noun for bees.
Printless Foot	Mysterious pedal complaint.
Grommet (also grummet, grumit, gromet, gromat, growbag, showbiz)	a) Complicated Elizabethan dance. b) An ill humour. As in *Separate Tables*. 'He was in a sorry grommet.'
Knap	To suddenly become. As in 'knap the rust' – to suddenly become angry. Or 'knap the dock-pheasant' – to suddenly become disillusioned. Or 'knap the Billy Turniptop' – to suddenly drop dead.
Culley-shangey	a) A post-prandial stroll. As in: 'Would you care for a quick *c-s* in the garden, my lady?' (*Macbeth* V; v; 123). b) Sexual intercourse. As in above.
Whap, whapper	Wrought-iron metal hook to hold door open when hot.

Folderol	Unexpected unpleasant odour in public place (see 'pomander').
Bozzy	Meaning unknown (prob. obscene).
Ludgate	Bill (as in restaurant). Rhym. sl. i.e. Ludgate Hill = Bill. As in *Antony and Cleopatra* V; iv; 507: 'Give me the ludgate forthwith, landlord!'
Methuen	Rare amphibious mammal, hunted for its sweet-scented hindquaters. As in *Hamlet* V; iv; 706: 'And let us hunt the sweet-scented methuen and snatch him in his caulfrey.'
Caulfrey	Nest of the methuen. Also used as base for a delicious soup.
St Gertrude of Nivelles	Daughter of Pepin of Landen.
Pomander	Orange carried near nose, to ward off sudden folderols. (See above.)
Ficky-fick	Meaning unknown (almost certainly obscene).
Groaty	Less popular rear part of pig's trotter.
Schlock	Inferior goods. As in *Merchant of Venice*: 'A load of old schlock, Bassanio!'
Potato Jack	Short-lived fluffy headpiece worn by men.
Silich!	Statement of utter disbelief. As in *Coriolanus* IV; iv; 908: 'The Queen and Lady Beaufort?' 'Yeah, my noble Lord!' 'Silich!'
Gravy	See faggot.
Dip the fly	Take a turn round the withdrawing room.
Yoo-hoo-boy	Front portion of pig's trotter.
Take a Brody	Go to the prithee. (See prithee.)
Reel in the biscuit	Popular Elizabethan wooing technique.
Gadfly	Rudimentary Renaissance zip.
Pintle-keek	Unusually small male member. As in *Julius Caesar* IV; iii; 654: 'Canst see his pintle-keek?'

	'No my lord!'
	'Exactly! Ha! Ha!'
Nuts, handful of	a) Painful wrestler's grip.
	b) Popular yuletide pleasure.
Boojum	See Snooks.
Chase the chubby	Popular Elizabethan wooing technique.
Soldier's Mawnd	Meaning unknown (prob. obsc.).
Snatch–blatch	Meaning unknown (prob. obsc.).
Rullock	Tasty freshwater fish (now extinct). As in *Othello* V; iv; 876: 'Thou art as young as rullock spawn, art not, Master Scrope?'
Cold pig, the	A feeling of profound dis-ease, e.g. To give someone the cold pig. As in *Pericles of Athens* IV; ii; 654: 'He just gave me the cold pig, my lady.'
Crumpet	Unusual Elizabethan pudding.

APPENDICES

'Bid the priest be ready
To come against you with your appendix.'

(Anon)

APPENDIX 1
Some Famed Shakespearean Theatres

The Globe
Donmar Warehouse
Billingham Forum
Olivier
Wembley Stadium
The Old Red Lion
Albery
Wyndhams
Palladium
Curzon

APPENDIX 2
Some Celebrated Shakespearean Actors

Mrs Siddons
Mrs Judi Dench
Mrs Juliet Stevenson
Sir Ian McKellen
Mrs Nyree Dawn Porter
Mrs Beeton
Lord Soames
Lady Susan Hampshire
The Rt Hon Jeremy Irons
Dame Pliant
Sir Oliver Martext
Mrs Warren
Sir Humphrey Bogard
Lord Gielgud
Lady Gregory
Sir John Suchet
Lady Windermere
Mr Peter Barkworth
Lord Charlton Heston

APPENDIX 3
The Publishing Dynasties of Britain at the Time of Shakespeare

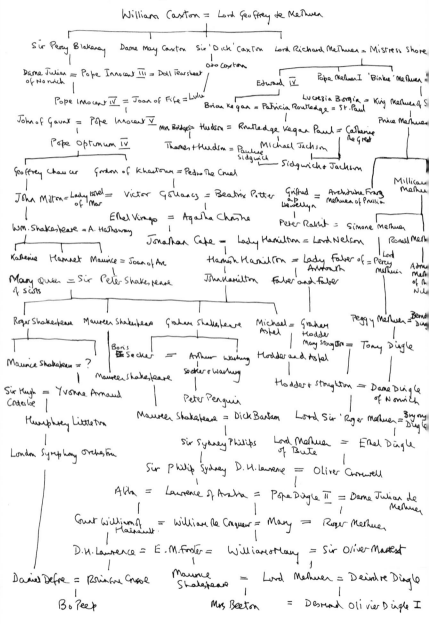

INDEX

THE END